Talking with the Trinity

Personally and Publicly

Carol J Slager

WESTBOW
PRESS®
A DIVISION OF THOMAS NELSON
& ZONDERVAN

WestBow Press books may be ordered through booksellers or by contacting:

WestBow Press
A Division of Thomas Nelson & Zondervan
1663 Liberty Drive
Bloomington, IN 47403
www.westbowpress.com
844-714-3454

ISBN: 978-1-6642-3291-4 (sc)
ISBN: 978-1-6642-3290-7 (e)

Print information available on the last page.

WestBow Press rev. date: 05/13/2021

I dedicate this book to

the precious women of my Bible 101 study.

May you forever pray,

trusting that God loves you, hears you,

and works through you to bless others.

He put you in my life as gifts of JOY.

CONTENTS

ACKNOWLEDGEMENTS

I am grateful for the many books, articles, lectures, sermons, and songs about prayer that have shaped my thinking, my heart, and my praying. Having had no life-long plan to write a book on prayer, I did not keep notes on those long-ago influences. This book arises out of my memory of those influences, my teaching of public speaking, my experiences praying, and especially my ongoing and growing understanding of the Trinity and prayer. My goal is to record for family, friends, and even strangers, the biblical meditations that impacted my faith as well as the visuals that I often use to illustrate my relationship with the Trinity and my loving desire to talk with Them. I chose not to research other's writings on prayer, desiring this volume to be personal. I was delighted when the Spirit stimulated my thoughts with Sunday sermons or daily devotions, and those have been noted and credited. My key reference was the Bible.

I invite interested readers to visit the books and websites listed below. I have found them to be inspiring and helpful in living a life of faith and prayer.

Bible Gateway (https://biblegateway.com), a division of the Zondervan Corporation
Use the search engine to pull up all Bible verses in which a searched word appears, in any Bible version desired.

Dictionary of Biblical Imagery, An encyclopedic exploration of the images, symbols, motifs, metaphors, figures of speech and literary patterns of the Bible edited by Leland Ryken, James C. Wilhoit, and Tremper Longman III, (InterVarsity Press, 1998)
The authors trace metaphors and images from the Old Testament through the New Testament.

Keep Believing Ministries with Dr. Ray Pritchard
(https://keepbelieving.com)
This ministry provides sermons, lecture series, and daily email thoughts.

Ligonier Ministries (https://ligonier.org)
This site offers devotionals and articles by R. C. Sproul and his associates, helping to tune Reformed thinking.

Michael Card (https://michaelcard.com)
Card's *Biblical Imagination* series and his creative expressions of biblical imagery in his songs have helped my faith to grow and my heart to rejoice.

Modesto Christian Reformed Church (https://modestocrc.org)
My faith has been shaped over fifty years by sermons, studies, conversations, and prayers from and with the pastors and congregants of this church. Presently, the words of Pastor Randy Beumer and Pastor Reese VanderVeen inspire me. Prayers by several members are included in this volume. Worship services including congregational prayers can be accessed on Youtube.

The NIV Serendipity BIBLE for Study Groups, edited by Lyman Coleman *et al,* (Zondervan Bible Publishers, 1989)
Questions in the margins of this Bible are insightful, connecting the biblical narrative and probing the believer's heart.

Prayers by Michel Quoist,
translated by Agnes M. Forsyth and Anne Marie de Commaille, (Sheed & Ward, 1963)
I encountered this collection of prayers while in college. Quoist deeply and poetically connects God into everyday experiences.

The Praying Church Idea Book by Douglas A. Kamstra,
(Faith Alive Resources/CRC Publications, 2001)
This resource describes many prayer templates such as *lectio divina* and breath prayers.

Sensible Shoes, A Story About the Spiritual Journey
by Sharon Garlough Brown, (IVP, 2013)
This fiction book (one in a series of four) follows several women who meet on a spiritual retreat. Their spiritual mentor shares many patterns for prayer, such as "palms up/palms down" and labyrinth walks.

Word on Fire: *Daily Gospel Reflections* by Bishop Robert Barron (https://wordonfire.org)
As a Protestant, I am uplifted by Bishop Barron's videos and daily emails articulating our universal faith. He is a wordsmith, expounding the Word and biblical imagery.

Your Journey to a Prayerful Life by Barbara Schutt,
(Chalice Press, 2009)
A comprehensive study of the Bible's teachings on prayer. I heard Barbara speak at a women's retreat, and I later led several small groups using her book as the basis of our study.

THANKSGIVING

Thank you to all who have commented with appreciation or critique on my public prayers. The encouragement of friends to collect and publish those prayers provided the impetus for writing this book.

Thank you to teacher-colleague, Sylvia Hannink, who in a long-ago chapel talk scanned the Scriptures, awakening my desire to understand and consistently reflect on the Bible in its wholeness. Thank you to those who read drafts of this book and bravely suggested changes: Brian Aird, Brent Folkerts, Cindy Slager Loacker, and Ron Vander Molen. Thank you to Lorna Van Gilst for her diligent editing and to Bruce Brown for preparing my photos and for sharing photos.

Precious Holy Spirit, Thank You for inspiring Your Word and for making it so accessible. Thank You for waking me with surprising thoughts and for staying with me in this endeavor. Thank You for leading me to hear and read words along the way that resonated with this topic and encouraged me to keep going. Thank You for editing my writing through Your quiet urgings and purgings. I love You, LORD. Be glorified in these words, I pray. Amen.

Note regarding capitalization of *pronouns*

To honor the majesty of God, I have chosen to capitalize all pronouns related to the Persons of the Trinity. However, when I write about Jesus during His time on earth, because He was willing to "give up His glory" to become human, I have chosen to use lower-case pronouns, indicating He was human with us.

Labyrinth in Trinity Garden
Trinity Episcopal Church, 44 N. 2nd Street, Ashland, OR

INTRODUCTION

I believe that all people pray. Praying is simply a verbal way that humans reach out to God. I suppose that even unbelievers and atheists unknowingly connect with God when they exclaim or curse using His name or write acronyms that reference Him. Praying, with or without heart commitment, is an astounding action that unites earth and heaven. When humans pray, we are connecting with the *living* God Who *listens*, with the *loving* God Who desires *relationship*, and with the *sovereign* God Who accomplishes with *power*.

Before we were ever created, this living God existed as Three-in-One: Father, Son, and Spirit. We often call this Trinity by one name, *God*, because Father, Son, and Spirit are one mind and one heart, working in harmony and communicating for one purpose. As One, They create and rule over the world and its creatures. As One, they create mankind, redeeming and elevating humans to be in loving relationship with Them. As One, They call us into partnership with Them to care for our neighbors and the world.

The Trinity enables us to communicate with Them and with others verbally and non-verbally. We receive truths from the Trinity about Them and Their purposes from four sources—through the glories of creation spoken into existence by God's Word, through God's Word the Bible, through the presence of God's Word in the person of Jesus on earth, and through the indwelling of the Holy Spirit Who confirms God's Word in believer's hearts. (As Christ's church testifies of these sources, its members, too, become sharers of truth.) Although the Trinity already knows everything about us, They invite us to converse with Them through prayer.

The first half of this book explores what the Bible teaches about our precious interactive relationship with the Trinity and how relying on prayer is an essential tool to help us work with Them and with our fellow humans.

We are privileged to pray both privately and publicly. **Private** prayers may happen spontaneously or develop in more disciplined ways as each of us seeks our Creator. Private prayers may be as simple as short gasping cries of joy, relief, frustration, desperation, or awe: *"Thank you!" "Whoa, Lord, that was a close one!" "Help me, Lord!" "Give me wisdom!" "But why, Lord?" "Lord, please!" "What? Wait! No!" "What a glorious sunset!" "Wow!"* It is likely that the longer we live in faith, the lengthier and more thoughtful our private prayers will become. Many will be led into deep conversations with God to discuss His power and His will to guide and to help, whether they are handling the relationships and events of their lives or meditating on the Word or simply pondering their days. Some believers will keep journals in which they write private letters to God to clarify thoughts and feelings, often interspersing questions with confessions, laments with praise, and requests with commitments. Such one-on-One prayerful interactions are convicting, therapeutic and renewing (See Appendix A). However, while I recognize that private prayers are essential to a life of faith, they are not the focus of this book.

Rather, Part Two of this book focuses on **public** prayers prayed to God *for others while those others are listening in.* These prayers happen on social media, during church services, and as a precious part of many group activities when people of faith gather. Many Christians are immersed in communities that provide Christian gatherings. Prayers in Christian community happen in Christian *homes* when prayers are spoken before meals, before bedtime, and to surround family decisions and struggles; in Christian *schools* when prayer begins and ends the day or blesses student activities; in Christian *churches* during worship and in *small groups and classes* when prayers begin and end the meetings; in Christian *social situations* when prayers enter into the celebration or grief; and on *social media* when fellow believers pray with each other.

Some Christians live in situations or areas of the country that isolate them from rich Christian community. For such believers, the suggestions and prayers in the second half of this book may seem unnecessary. However, it is my hope that Part Two will provide all Christians with inspiration and encouragement to pray publicly within their *family and friendship gatherings* as well as on their *social media* posts. Part Two offers suggestions for creating public prayers, provides examples of them, and invites the reader to worship God while meditating on the prayers provided.

It is my hope that believers will be quick to pray, bringing friends and neighbors into the presence of our Three-in-One-God. May we talk to God—often and freely—with trust and hope—on earth as it is in heaven—about everything.

CJS

Part One

Talking with the Trinity
Personally

He will cover you with his feathers,
And under his wings you will find refuge...

"Because he loves me," says the LORD, "I will rescue him;
I will protect him, for he acknowledges my name.
He will call upon me, and I will answer him;
I will be with him in trouble,
I will deliver him and honor him.
With long life will I satisfy him
and show him my salvation."

Psalm 91:4, 14-16, *NIV*

MY PRAYER JOURNEY

I was created in the womb of a praying mother. After God breathed life into me, my days were swaddled in the prayer habits of our family. As soon as my brother and I could talk, Mother helped us memorize bedtime prayers. As young children, we were occasionally asked to offer a prayer of our own making before the meal. I can see myself peeking through my fingers at the food on the table and thanking God for the applesauce. Because table prayer was also the habit of my relatives, meals at their homes reinforced my prayer training. I can still hear Uncle John's voice, stretching out the vowels of his memorized prayer into a rolling song of faith: "Lord God, Heavenly Father, bless these gifts we are about to receive through Thy bountiful goodness in Christ Jesus our Lord. Amen." We prayed in church and we prayed in Sunday school. We never left the house on a road-trip vacation without first reading Psalm 121 and praying for safety.

When I was eight, we moved to a new town and I began to attend a Christian school. My teacher asked her students to take turns praying before lunches. I recall the first lunchtime prayer I heard there, a classmate asking God to "forgive our sins of omission and commission." I had no idea what she was talking about, but I remember desperately wanting such impressive words in my prayer vocabulary. (However, I can attest without regret, that although I now understand their meanings, I have *never* used those words to pray about sin.)

These experiences were vital to my growing faith. They gave me confidence to speak with God out loud. Yet, although I loved God and prayed to Him from my earliest years, I see now that I didn't understand the power of those prayer conversations until I was forty—when I had an encounter with God that changed all that.

***

In 1987, I bought a new car, choosing to sell on my own my old, dented, red Pontiac Sunbird with yellow pin-stripes. Friends allowed me to park the car on their property which fronted the heavily-trafficked Highway 120. After three months, I finally got a call of interest. Inexperienced at car selling, I met the family at the car, recklessly allowed them to test-drive it without me riding along, and gladly took their money when they (thankfully!) returned to purchase it. The next day, I went to the DMV to report that the car was no longer mine.

"Please write down the name and address of the buyer on the pink slip," the DMV clerk said.

What? "I don't have that information!" I said, troubled.

"Well, then, you'll need to keep insurance on the vehicle, because it will stay registered to you, and you're liable for it."

Shocked and shaken, I left the DMV and climbed into my new car considering my options: I could lie—I could make up a buyer's name and address, since I didn't trust that the buyers would be registering the car anyway. I could keep paying insurance on two cars. I could go in search of my car. As silly as the last option seemed, that is what I chose to do. I was crying. I knew only God could help me. *Lord, I have no idea where those people live! Yesterday they drove the car west to test drive it, so they might live in Manteca, but they might live east in Escalon. Of course, they might not live anywhere near there at all! Please, help me find them! Okay, okay—I'm going to go to Escalon, and drive up and down all the streets, looking for my red car with the yellow stripes.*

I gassed up the car and drove the ten miles to Escalon. After turning up and down just three side-streets, it became apparent that my plan was ludicrous. The red car with yellow pin-stripes could be in any garage, behind any barn, or the new owners could be out of town for the day! Weeping, I cried out loud, "Lord! I can't drive up and down every street in the county! But I *have* to find them! I can't carry insurance on *two* cars! Please help me!"

A thought popped into my mind. My friends who lived on the ranch where the car had been parked had not been home the day I had sold the car, but I had told the buyers that those friends had the extra car key. I had suggested the buyers could return the next day to get it. *Perhaps the buyers would stop by, and my friends could get their name and address!*

I headed down Highway 120 toward my friends' house; however, as I approached, I could see a number of flashing lights and emergency-vehicles. An accident had closed the highway between me and my friends' place! I was forced to turn left onto Jack Tone Road. "Okay, Lord! What am I supposed to do now?!?"

I drove two miles down Jack Tone and was nearing the interstate. "I'm going home to Modesto," I sighed out loud. "I'll call my friends from home and tell them about the key. I don't know what else to do."

That's when I "heard" it—it was not a voice; there was no sound, but to my brain there was an urging like a voice.

Go to Manteca.

I responded out loud, flabbergasted, "Go to Manteca? Turn onto the highway and go to Manteca? And do what? I don't know Manteca!"

Go to Manteca.

"Augh...gh! Okay! I'll go!" (In retrospect, I am amazed that I believed the urging was real and obeyed it as if it were a person.) Doubtful and sighing, I turned away from home onto the highway entrance ramp towards Manteca. Being familiar with only the Moffet exit into Manteca (which no longer exists), I took it.

By the time Moffet Road dead-ended into Manteca's Main Street, I had formed a plan. I would turn right and drive through *every* store parking lot along Main Street, looking for my red car with the yellow stripes. I turned and drove for blocks, going in and out of parking lots, searching up and down rows of cars. I reached the end of Main Street. Nothing.

"Okay, Lord, it's hopeless! My car isn't here. I'm going home."

I turned around, retracing my route, and pulled into the left turn-lane to head down Yosemite Avenue to the highway. The light was red and I waited.

Go right.

"What? Go *right*? I'm in the left turn-lane!" Nevertheless, I checked my mirrors. There was no one behind me.

Go right.

Belligerently, I yanked the wheel, crossed two lanes, and turned right. I drove block after block, looking down every street on the driver's side for a red car with yellow stripes. Nothing.

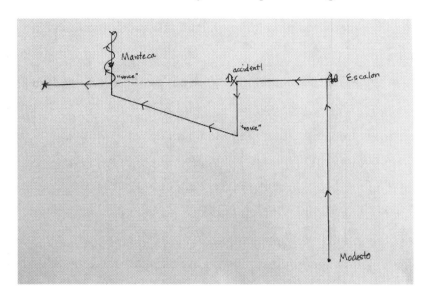

"This is ridiculous, Lord! I'm looking down all these streets, and You can see that there are lots of garages and stuff. How am I going to find my car in all that?"

I kept driving, bitter frustration curling my lip. Then, a thought came to my mind: *K-Mart is way down this road. Maybe the buyers and their children would be shopping at K-Mart at 2:30 in the afternoon.* I aimed for K-Mart.

Several blocks more and the K-Mart shopping center appeared on my right. I turned into the parking lot. There were rows and rows of parked cars. Slowly I maneuvered up and down each row, scanning the cars. My red Sunbird with yellow stripes was not there.

Angry and hopeless, I exploded, "Okay, that's it! I am going home!" I headed toward the shopping-center's exit by the Pizza Hut.

And that's when I saw it. My car. My red car with the yellow stripes. Heart jumping, breath catching, I slammed on the brakes. My red Sunbird with the yellow stripes was parked in front of the Pizza Hut! It was the *only* car parked in front of the Pizza Hut!

"My car! Oh, Lord! *My car!*" I gasped. "You *found* it! *You found it!*"

I pulled my new car in beside the red car with the yellow stripes and parked, staring at the Sunbird through the window in disbelief. Then, after turning off the engine, I fumbled in my purse to make sure I had paper and pen. I got out of the car and entered the Pizza Hut.

There were absolutely no customers inside—*except* for the lady to whom I had sold the car. She and her children were finished eating and were gathering their things to get up from the table. I walked over to them.

"Excuse me—hi! Do you remember me? I'm Carol—the lady from whom you bought the car yesterday? I forgot to get your name and address, and I need them for the pink slip. Would you mind writing them on this piece of paper?"

Somewhat surprised, but nodding, the lady silently took my paper and pen and immediately began to write the information, while her children stared at me. Suddenly the strangeness of the situation dawned on her. She stopped writing and looked up. "But, how did you *find* me?"

Grinning and holding back joyful tears, I shook my head in wonder and breathed out, "I didn't find you. *The LORD* found you! I just drove the car!"

If she thought me out of my mind, she didn't show it. She simply smiled, nodded, and saying nothing more, finished writing the information. She handed back the paper and pen. I thanked her, tucked them into my purse, and needing nothing more, I left.

Once outside, I sank into my new car, covered my face with my hands, and let the tears flow. "Oh, Lord! Thank You! *Thank You!* I'm so sorry; I shouldn't have doubted."

And then—it was the oddest sensation—I felt as if my car were full of giant, rather stiff and oily feathers and I was being hugged by them! It was real; it lasted only a moment, and then it was gone. I think of angels as having wings. Had I been dealing with an angel? I don't know, but I think so.

Where does one go after such an experience? I raced to my mom's apartment to recount what had happened! The next day, I went to the DMV and transferred the pink slip. And from that day on, I have been sharing the story.

I had prayed to God, yet argued with Him about the answers. I had asked for help, but doubted the directions. Nevertheless, Father had patiently stuck with me. The God Who creates and manages the great agenda of Glory was aware of one distraught wandering sheep in a little town on a road in northern California. With meticulous timing—the accident that kept me moving, the red light holding until I changed my direction, the woman just ready to leave the restaurant—He had given me the gift of answered prayer. He had helped a desperate, crying, belligerent child. He had *seen* my comings and goings, He had *heard* my cries.

***

It was because of that intimate experience that my faith catapulted and my prayer life began to change. Oh, I still am at times rebellious and I always need to confess my sins and seek the grace of God, but I know that I belong to a God Who hears me and answers my prayers. My trust in Him keeps growing and I talk with Him every day about what I see around me, about my major concerns as well as my minutia.

I have asked Him to bring to mind topics for speeches and ideas for speech visuals—and He has. I have asked Him to edit my prayers—and He does. When it was time to quit teaching, I pleaded for guidance to find other work and within a week He opened a job at my church. When I retired but needed mental stimulation, He pointed me to a part-time tutoring job. Some of my prayers are still waiting for His answers to be revealed, and to some of my prayers He has answered "no," but with hindsight, I am thankful for His "no's." He cares for me and is teaching me that sometimes I ask for the wrong things or sometimes I cling to control. At times I have launched a new venture without praying and I have suffered the consequences. Yet, I can testify with joy that the Spirit has ways of calling me back until I turn to seek His guidance.

I am delighted to testify to others about the tiny yet delightful ways He has responded to my prayers, such as providing help to find my keys or to find an accessible parking spot to aid my frail old friend or to find a picnic spot from which to see the ocean (See Appendix B). My prayers often are requests for God's help with immediate and small concerns. I now talk with God as if He is standing beside me and I call His attention to what I am wondering about or noticing or delighting in. My prayers are also for others as I become aware of their needs. While writing this book, I have come to sense that the Spirit is calling me to enlarge my awareness of social issues, to pray with larger scope for my country and the world. I am trying to answer that call.

When I was growing up, a ceramic plaque hung in our home. It read: "Prayer Changes Things." I recently learned that Mother Theresa embraced that statement, adding that prayer also "changes *us*." I agree. Prayer is precious face-time with Father, Son, and Holy Spirit. We seek Their gifts of grace, forgiveness, discernment, and power, while thanking Them for all they provide. We study Their Word, trusting in the mystery of Their will and Their timing. We seek to converse and work with Them to restore earth so that it reflects the Kingdom of heaven.

Garden of Gethsemane, Mount of Olives, Israel - 2012

FOCUSING ON FATHER

As a child, I was taught to recite prayers that focused on God the Father. Each morning at breakfast I prayed this prayer (author unknown):

> *Heavenly Father, be Thou near me.*
> *Make me gentle, kind, and true.*
> *Teach me to obey and serve Thee,*
> *love Thee best in all I do. Amen.*

Each lunch time I recited this prayer (author unknown):

> *God is great. God is good,*
> *and we thank Him for our food.*
> *By His hand we all are fed.*
> *Give us, Lord, our daily bread. Amen.*

Before supper my family would recite The Lord's Prayer (Mt. 6:9-13):

> *Our Father in heaven,*
> *hallowed be your name,*
> *your kingdom come,*
> *your will be done,*
> *on earth as it is in heaven.*
> *Give us today our daily bread.*
> *And forgive us our debts,*
> *as we also have forgiven our debtors.*
> *And lead us not into temptation,*
> *but deliver us from the evil one.*

Kneeling by my bed at night, I prayed this prayer which I understand first appeared in the 18th century *New England Primer*:

> *Now I lay me down to sleep.*
> *I pray the Lord my soul to keep.*
> *If I should die before I wake,*
> *I pray the Lord my soul to take. Amen.*

In addition to our prayer times, my parents read to us from a Bible storybook in which God the Father was always the Prime Mover—calling, rescuing, teaching, and sending out characters such as Adam and Eve, Noah, Abraham and Sarah, Jacob and Leah, Hagar, Moses, Hannah and Samuel, Samson, David, and Daniel.

My parents also brought my brothers and me to Sunday school classes, catechism classes, and worship services. We attended churches of the Reformed faith—a faith tradition awed by the sovereignty of God. In those churches I learned to praise Father because He is over all.

❖ It is Father Who designed this astoundingly diverse and beautiful creation.

❖ It is Father Whose power fills the earth—riding the clouds as His chariot, thundering from the stormy heavens, causing earthquakes, shattering rocks, surrounding Himself with wind and fire, flooding the earth and refreshing it with rain, ruining crops with locusts or bringing abundant harvests.

❖ It is Father who commands angel hosts and the cherubim and seraphim.

❖ It is Father Whose authority puts the evil one in his place; installs and removes leaders; brings nations to ruin; calls people to repentance and offerings, obedience and holiness; and establishes His Kingdom.

❖ It is Father Who sends Jesus and tells Jesus what to say.

❖ It is Father Who loves His children—disciplining their wayward ways, providing food with miraculous bounty, healing their diseases, forgiving their sins, and raising them from the dead.

❖ It is Father Who proliferates and protects His people—opening and closing their wombs, releasing them from captivity and jail cells, fighting their enemies, leading them through the wilderness, and pointing them to mission for the world.

Of course, I also learned about Jesus and the Holy Spirit. I knew that the Holy Spirit was leading me to follow Jesus Who loved me and died for me, but in my younger years, my faith and prayers were focused on honoring Father. I developed a deep respect for His will and I trusted His leading. I aimed my prayers at Him, even though He was a Father I had never seen.

FATHER'S BODY

There is a saying: *Seeing is believing.* No one wants to fall victim to a fantasy; we want the facts. We want to see the realities. So, too, did the disciple Thomas. He had missed Jesus' first appearance to the disciples, leaving Thomas skeptical about Jesus' resurrection, but his skepticism didn't last long. When Jesus appeared to the disciples a second time, he spoke directly to Thomas, "Because you have seen me, you have believed; blessed are those who have not seen and yet have believed" (John 20:29). Those words are echoed in a later biblical teaching: "Now faith is confidence in what we hope for and assurance about what we do not see" (Heb. 11:1).

Isn't it fascinating that although many people of the Bible spoke with Father or received messages from Him or saw the works of His mighty hands, almost none of them provided a physical description of Father? Adam and Eve were so close to God that they received the breath of life from His nostrils, and they walked and talked with God in the Garden, yet no description of God's appearance is given (Gen. 1, 2). Theologians believe that the pre-incarnated Jesus appeared as the "angel of the LORD" speaking to such people as Hagar (Gen. 16:7-14) and Abraham (Gen. 18), but neither account describes Him. Exodus 33:11 records that "The LORD would speak to Moses face to face, as one speaks to a friend," but goes on to record the LORD saying, "You cannot see my face, for no one may see me and live" (Ex. 33:20), so Moses is allowed to see the back of Father as He passes (Ex. 33:23), but even Father's back is not described. The prophet Isaiah sees the Lord seated on the throne in a robe, but does not describe His body.

Perhaps the most tantalizing descriptions of God are when He appears in His glory. "The glory of the LORD" is a recurring phrase used for God sightings—awesome displays of light, fire and cloud—as when God gives the law on Mt. Sinai or when He is leading the Israelites through the wilderness or when He appears in the tabernacle and the Temple. We can't comprehend such awesome glory, but Ezekiel and John both record shining visions of a figure:

> High above on the throne was a figure like that of a man. I saw that from what appeared to be his waist up he looked like glowing metal, as if full of fire, and that from there down he looked like fire; and brilliant light surrounded him. Like the appearance of a rainbow in the clouds on a rainy day, so was the radiance around him. This was the appearance of the likeness of the glory of the LORD.
>
> (Ez. 1:26a-28b)

> Someone like a son of man, dressed in a robe reaching down to his feet and with a golden sash around his chest. The hair on his head was white like wool, as white as snow, and his eyes were like blazing fire. His feet were like bronze glowing in a furnace . . . and coming out of his mouth was a sharp, double-edged sword. His face was like the sun shining in all its brilliance.
>
> (Rev. 1:13-16)

Clearly, God is not one of His creatures, so it is hard to comprehend why people would cast the Almighty Creator into a paltry creature's image of wood or stone and worship that, but many did. It was so common that God warned against it (Ex. 20:4-6).

Even without seeing His Person, certainly all of these visions and displays of God's awesome acts of provision and protection should be more than sufficient to satisfy our desire to "see" God. They call forth praise and worship and prayers, and the triple "Holy, holy, holy!" of Revelation 4:8. Nevertheless, we continue to desire to peruse Him. Having created human beings as visualizing creatures, Father seems to understand this. In His grace and mercy, God allowed Spirit-led biblical authors, especially the prophets and the song writers, to employ a plethora of familiar *imagery* to describe Him.

King David was inspired to write songs and prayers in which he imagined a body for God; Psalm 17 is a good example. Meditating on an embodied God must have comforted David and built his confidence as he hid out in caves, fought his enemies, and ruled his people. David's imagery focuses on God's head and arms, quite unlike the genitalia focus we see in excavated idols (or our own culture's fascination with torsos.) Perhaps David was remembering how as a parent he had held a baby or how as a shepherd he had held a lamb. In the arms of the parent/shepherd, the infant wriggles and bleats, seeking to focus on its caretaker's face, mouth, and eyes; seeking to listen to its caretaker's voice; seeking to know that the caretaker holds it secure and protected. Like an infant, David prays to be heard and seen, to have his hand held and to be hidden close to God. Additionally, David creates pictures of rescue and justice in which he describes God in terms that suggest our modern day super heroes—a God who reaches down with his mighty arms to pull David up from the miry pit, Who earnestly fights all enemies until He is victorious, Who even seems to transform into a terrifying, fire-breathing Warrior taking down all who oppose Him (Ps. 18:8-16).

If we fit David's references together like the pieces of a jigsaw puzzle, we can claim Father's promises as we imagine and visualize Father from head to foot (emphasis forward, mine):

> Father turns his **face** toward us and shines on us
> (Num. 6:25-26). His **eyes** see everything and watch
> over us (Ps. 121:3-5,7-8). His **ears** hear our cries for

> help (Ps. 17:6). His **nostrils** smell the incense of our
> sacrifice and when He breathes from His nostrils,
> He can part the sea (Ps. 18:15). His voice/**mouth**
> controls the world (Ps. 33:6). His **arm** is strong to
> save his people (Ps 77:15). Our times are in His
> **hands** (Ps. 31:15); His **right hand** will rescue us and
> satisfy us with good things (Ps. 108:6; 104:27-28).
> His **wings** shelter us so that we may sing (Ps. 63:7).
> His **feet** are firmly planted in the depths of the sea
> and He will trample on our enemies.
>
> (Ps. 77:19; Ps. 108:13).

Bringing to mind this head-to-toe imagery of God can provide a powerful template for our prayers, an outline within which we may thank Father for His goodness or plead upon His promises. I have suggested to aged believers and deployed military who may not have easy access to the Word that they recall these truths by simply touching their face, eyes, ears, nose, mouth, arm, hand, shoulder, and feet. While Biblical writers' meager personifications fall far short of God's splendor and power, their pictures do help our human minds connect with Father.

Of course, the good news of the gospels is that in His perfect timing, God *did* appear in a way that allowed us to see Him and believe. Father sent His Son Jesus—His exact representation—to live among us (John 1:18; 14:9)! Jesus was fully human—he walked, ate, slept, spoke, listened, touched, worked, wept, played, laughed, prayed, and worshipped just like us—but he never sinned. Yet, though he was on earth for thirty-three years, isn't it intriguing that the only physical description we have of Jesus is found in the prophecy of Isaiah 53:2b where the coming one is described as having "no beauty or majesty to attract us to him, / nothing in his appearance that we should desire him." Such a mundane appearance for the glorious God! And therefore, how amazing the experience of Peter, James, and John—seeing God's divine glory shining forth from Jesus' earthly body at his Transfiguration: "His face shone like the sun, and his clothes became as white as the light" (Mt 17: 2). John writes later:

> We have seen his glory, the glory of the one and only Son, who came from the Father, full of grace and truth . . . . No one has ever seen God, but the one and only Son, who is Himself God and is at the Father's side, has made Him known.
>
> (John 1:14, 18)

Rather than admire his body, we are asked to turn our eyes upon Jesus and remember the horrific desecration and death of his body that resulted in our salvation. Spit upon, mocked, stripped, flogged, nailed to a cross, and pierced, his body lost life and was buried. He became the final slaughtered Lamb, taking the place of all the unblemished perfect lambs of the Old Testament that were sacrificed for sin. This is our Savior! This is our Lord! This is the One to Whom we may pray! Given resurrection life, he arose victorious from the grave. His resurrected body, though looking familiar, evidenced powers his disciples had never seen before, such as the ability to enter locked rooms and cover distances quickly. After appearing to many in the flesh, Jesus ascended into heaven and in that body that bears his crucifixion scars (Rev. 5:6), He is seated in glory at the right hand of Father. From there, Jesus prays for us continually.

What a perfect Mediator! Having experienced our human condition in the flesh yet without sin, He fully understands when we pray to Him about our joys or our sorrows. He fully understands who we are and what we experience. Our hope is in Him; our bodies, too, will rise and live with Him face-to-face.

However, until we leave for heaven, there is yet one more important way that Father can be seen to be believed. After dying for our sins and rising to reign with Father, Jesus sent His Spirit to live within the Church, *transforming believers to be His Body* on earth (I Cor. 12:27, Eph. 1:22-23). Humans don't become little gods, but we are transformed by God's power, able to talk with the Trinity daily about how we can demonstrate the goodness and shalom of the Kingdom. Washed by the blood of the Lamb and resurrected to new life by His Spirit, we can joyfully testify about God and share His Word to make Him known. We can shine with God's light (Mt. 5:16), imitate Him (Eph. 5:1), declare His praises (I Pet. 2:9), and become living sacrifices "holy and pleasing to God" (Rom. 12:1). People can "see" Father in believers who live out the Word, testify of Christ, and pray for others and the world.

FATHER—THE COVENANTING GOD

Praying arises out of a firm conviction—or a desperate hope—that there is a *living* God who *listens* and *acts*. When we pray, we are seeking to connect with Him. For believers, this connection develops as they read the Word which reveals Father and provides a record of fellow humans who witnessed Father's great actions, who talked directly with Father or who were taught His purposes through prophets, and whose hearts drew them nearer to Father (or kept them away from Him.) In the Bible, the Spirit records these relationships and these conversations with Father. Face-to-face, or earth-space to heaven-space, these conversations are models for prayer, for dialoguing with God.

Long ago my heart was captured by seminary lectures presenting the biblical record of *covenant* conversations between Father and biblical characters. When making covenant, Father offers His lavish love and grace (Eph 1:7-8); He offers a loving relationship with all its blessings and missions, an intimate relationship in which we can delight and dialogue, work and worship.

Father chose us and initiates this relationship of love, honor, purity, exclusivity of heart, and faithfulness (Eph 1: 4-6). Because He is always faithful, He is upfront in telling us covenant partners that His name is Jealous (Ex. 34:14; 20:5). If idols or other gods capture our affections, He can claim His right to become angry and to exercise the option of avenging His honor. Therefore, after His Spirit calls us into covenant and we humbly receive that invitation, both of us *vow* to keep up the loving relationship. No matter what happens, we promise that we will seek first what is best for our partner—that is our covenant.

God shaped His covenants in the Bible using a treaty template with which the Israelites were familiar, that of the Ancient Near Eastern treaties. These treaties were often sealed with *blood oaths* that involved cutting or piercing. (The word *covenant* roots in a Hebrew word that meant *to cut*.) These bloody self-maledictory oaths were "visual curses" designed to mean, "may I *die* in such-and-such a way, if I don't keep my promises in this relationship." (As a child, you may have participated in something like these oaths. Perhaps you promised to be a "blood brother or sister" with a friend, each of you pricking a finger to get a drop of blood and touching your bloody fingers together as a sign of "loyalty forever.") Of course, God can't die, but men understood how serious Father was about the covenant relationship when He took such an oath or required it of them. Father wanted to provide safety, surety, and love. Throughout the Old Testament, we see Father providing or requiring blood oaths to seal covenant relationships—with Noah and the world (the rainbow), with Abraham (split animals, the ram replacing Isaac as sacrifice, circumcision), with Moses and the Israelites (the sacrificial system). He confirms his covenant with David (successful wars) and brings it to fulfillment in Jesus (the cross). (See Appendix C to more fully reference the Bible's bloody trail of promises.)

Sadly, we humans are prone to unfaithfulness and selfishness. After the devil brought doubt and selfish desire into the Garden, human experience became an ongoing struggle of either staying faithful to God or prostituting our hearts by following the idols of the world, our fleshly ways, and the devil. We corrupt the covenant relationship with self-centeredness when our hearts believe that the world revolves around us or that we deserve God's good gifts or that we earn our place in God's kingdom through religious practices and good works or that we need not consult with God in prayer. Covenant unfaithfulness occurs whenever we seek ultimate identity, meaning, joy and hope in anything but Him.

Thankfully, Father sends His Word and Spirit to urgently warn us when dangers are near, when plans are going awry, when selfishness and wandering are tearing our covenant apart. He assures us that in Him shalom and joy can prevail and flourish. He passionately calls us back—even going out to seek us, find us, and bring us home—because ending covenant is not God's plan for His relationships (Jer. 3:12-14). The Apostle Peter writes, "He is patient with you, not wanting anyone to perish, but everyone to come to repentance" (2 Pet. 3:9). Father will do anything of good purpose to bring us back into loving and faithful relationship with Him. Grace, mercy, forgiveness, and restoration are His ways of working (Hos. 1-6). His Spirit is eager to lead us into earnest prayers of confession and recommitment:

> Have mercy on me, O God,
>   according to your unfailing love;
> according to your great compassion
>   blot out my transgressions. . . .
> You desired faithfulness. . . .
> Restore to me the joy of your salvation
>   and grant me a willing spirit,
>   to sustain me.
>   (Ps. 51:1, 6a, 12)

Nevertheless, if we continue to behave with hard hearts, maligning His Name and His holiness and disrespecting His power, His nature must seek justice (Ex. 20: 2-7). Father's nature is perfect goodness and holiness; He cannot blink at, tolerate, or live in union with evil and hate. Initially He may aim His wrath and destruction at the evils with which we cohort. Then He will aim His discipline at us, His unfaithful covenant partners. Sometimes He may exile us or allow trials in our lives so that our hearts will yearn for Him and we will spurn evil (Jer. 5:19). Ultimately, unless Father's beloved ones seek and find a Savior, the holy God will judge and destroy whomever and whatever insists on clinging to evil (Acts 17:30-31, Rev. 14:9-11). Such destruction must break the Creator's heart.

THE METAPHOR OF MARRIAGE

Throughout the Bible, a key way our covenant relationship with God is pictured is as a marriage covenant (Is. 62:5, Jer. 2:2; 3:14; Ez. 16:8-14; Mt. 9:15; Eph. 5:25). "For your Maker is your husband, the LORD of hosts is his name; and the Holy One of Israel is your Redeemer, the God of the whole earth he is called" (Is. 54:5). This analogy initiates with the Father's love and is carried forward by the Son. Before the creation of the world, the Almighty King chose us (Eph 1:4) and gifted us with His sovereign love and His wonderful gifts and promises. Believers are to be His Son's faithful bride, His passionate Church, His honoring confidant. We are to partner with Him and enjoy Him and together skillfully plan how to fulfill Father's good purposes.

Father sent His Son to be the Bridegroom. Jesus' perfect life demonstrates how to keep Father's covenant expectations. Jesus reminded us of Father's heart—to love Him above all and our neighbors as ourselves (Mt. 22:36-40). Despite repeated calls to be faithful, our faithless hearts ruined the hopes of a good union (Jer. 31:32), until our Bridegroom took our place on the cross, alone and forsaken by Father, suffering the agony of the bloody death curse caused by our broken "if-I-don't-keep-my-half-of-the-covenant-may-I-die" oath. His blood brought renewed hope, sealing again the promises and the new oaths of God's renewed covenant—Father's promise of forgiving love and mankind's promise of obedient love.

> For you know that it was not with perishable things such as silver or gold that you were redeemed from the empty way of life handed down to you from your ancestors, but **with the precious blood of Christ,** a lamb without blemish or defect. He was chosen before the creation of the world, but was revealed in these last times for your sake.
>
> (I Pet. 1:18-20)

To keep us mindful of our relationship as we approach the wedding day, Jesus instructs us to be *baptized* in the name of the Father, Son, and Holy Spirit. Baptism reminds us of God's gracious love, freeing us from sin; it calls us to honor the name, family, and Kingdom we are taking on; and it points us to grow through the Word and Spirit (Mt. 28:19-20; John 3:5; Acts 2:38; Col 2:12-13; 1 Cor 12:13)). Baptism strengthens our understanding of the vow of "holy matrimony."

Jesus also invites us to regularly dine with Him at the table of the *Lord's Supper*, to remember during this intimate, sobering, yet joyfully assuring celebration what he sacrificed to bring us into covenant life with Him. Matthew 26: 26-28 says:

> Jesus took bread, and when he had given thanks, he broke it and gave it to his disciples, saying, "Take and eat; this is my body."
>
> Then he took a cup, and when he had given thanks, he gave it to them, saying, "Drink from it, all of you. This is my blood of the covenant, which is poured out for many for the forgiveness of sins."

At her wedding, a Jewish bride signifies her willingness to enter into the marriage covenant by accepting and drinking from the cup of wine her husband offers. So, too, we pledge ourselves to covenant holiness and faithfulness when we accept the wine, drink it, and eat the bread offered by Jesus at His table.

As we anticipate the wedding day of the Lamb with His Church, the day when heaven will unite with earth forevermore, the day when what God has joined together can no longer be torn apart, we eagerly talk to others about our Bridegroom. We testify of His great love and of the love of the Father Who perfected the covenant through Jesus' blood. Jesus has been called home to reign and is in heaven continually praying for us (Heb. 7:25), talking with Father about us. Not wanting to leave His beloved alone, He has sent His Spirit, to live with us, prepare us, and seal our relationship (Eph. 4:30). The Spirit is intimately writing Father's covenant expectations on our hearts (2 Cor. 3:3) and is working to make us radiant (Rev. 19:6-8a). Every day He is willing to help us connect with Jesus through prayer, because, after all, who of us would not want to talk with our Bridegroom and His family about everything, planning into the future with Them and sharing our love?

IN THE NAME OF JESUS

I am fascinated by the Bible's frequent use of the little word *in*. Although it is an often-used preposition, it can intentionally carry profound meaning in the Word. The Spirit drew my attention to the word *in* during that same year God helped me find my red car with the yellow stripes. I had been asked to speak at a retreat for a Christian girls' club called GEMS (Girls Everywhere Meeting the Savior). Their theme verse for the year was:

> Do not be anxious about anything, but in every situation, by prayer and petition, with thanksgiving, present your requests to God. And the peace of God, which transcends all understanding, will guard your hearts and minds in Christ Jesus.
>
> (Phil. 4:6-7)

My attention was drawn to the closing phrase. What did it mean to have a heart and mind guarded *in Christ Jesus*? How might I explain and illustrate that?

The visuals that came to mind were a blanket and a sponge. I used the blanket to remind the girls that prepositions show *relationship* and *position*. I asked them to demonstrate "*by* the blanket," "*under* the blanket," "*on* the blanket," "*near* the blanket." When I asked them to demonstrate "*in* the blanket," they did their best by enfolding themselves within the blanket since they couldn't weave themselves into the substance of the blanket. When we say we are "*in* love," "*in* debt," "*in* doubt," "*in* haste," we're all clear on what is meant; we're not saying that we have "become one" with love, debt, doubt, or haste, but we're feeling quite engulfed or overwhelmed by what is named.

However, when the Bible speaks of believers being *in Christ* and He *in us*, the reference does suggest becoming one; it carries great intimacy. I didn't ask the GEMS girls to consider this, but in what ways is it possible for people to be *in* other creatures? We may clothe ourselves with skins or put on costumes to assume another's identity, but we aren't *in* a living creature. Many people put other creatures *in* themselves as they eat them, but what we eat is usually dead and in pieces, and thankfully, not human. (Remember that pagans in ancient times accused believers of cannibalism because they spoke of eating the body and drinking the blood of Christ.) Perhaps the truest image of person-to-person "*in*timacy" would be sexual intimacy within the covenant bond of marriage. Genesis 2:24 says the man and woman "become one flesh." Ephesians 5:31-32 echoes this as a metaphor when speaking of the "great mystery of Christ and His church."

Not physical intimacy, but rich and fulfilling spiritual intimacy is what I believe the Bible most often intends. The Bible does not usually record that we "trust God," "believe God," "have faith," and "rejoice." No, the Bible most often states that we "trust *in* God," "believe *in* God," "have faith *in* Him," and "rejoice *in* the Lord." The Psalms and writings of Paul are filled with such phrases. The presence of that little word suggests that we don't engage in these actions alone using simply human power. No, we act in conjunction with God; we are invited and pulled into being one with the Three-in-One (Acts 17:28). When we are *in* God, we are embraced and enveloped by His overwhelming love, His strong security, and His complete understanding. The word suggests *partnership.*

So it is that we don't "pray the name," as if His name were some abracadabra word—*Jesus! Jesus! Jesus!* The Apostle Paul ran into men attempting that, but it didn't go well for them (Acts 19:13-17). We don't shoot our prayers like arrows across a great distance hoping they will penetrate the doors of heaven, hoping God might take time to listen. No, "*in* Jesus' name" and with hearts that have covenanted with Him and have been redeemed by His blood, we gather at the Trinity "family table", so to speak, to talk with Them, laughing and crying, learning and deliberating (emphasis forward, mine).

> God raised us up with Christ and seated us with him
> in the heavenly realms **in Christ Jesus**, in order that
> in the coming ages he might show the incomparable
> riches of his grace, expressed in his kindness to us

in Christ Jesus. . . . For through him we both have access to the Father by one Spirit."

(Eph 2: 6-7, 18)

Father delights to welcome and unite men and women of every tribe and nation, of every economic and social status, because we are clothed *in* the righteousness of Jesus:

> So **in Christ Jesus** you are all children of God through faith, for all of you who were baptized into Christ have **clothed** yourselves with Christ. There is neither Jew nor Gentile, neither slave nor free, nor is there male and female, for you are all one **in Christ Jesus**.
>
> (Gal.3:26-28)

If synthetic sponges had existed in the Apostle Paul's day, he might have added sponge imagery into his writings. Synthetic sponges helpfully illustrate how we are *in Christ*. Imagine a modern-day dry, hard sponge lying on a dry surface. It is so dry that when a puff of air comes, it skitters away like chaff in the wind; but place it near liquid and it will soak up whatever it contacts – clear water, slop water, poisonous liquids, alcohol. Once a sponge soaks up dirty water, it can't become clean again until it is dunked and squeezed and dunked and rinsed in purifying water. So it is with us. Outside of Christ, we are often blown away by life's temptations and troubles (Eph. 4:14) and are prone to soak up sin; the Apostle Paul suggests this when he writes: "Count yourselves dead to sin but alive to God **in Christ Jesus.** Therefore do not let sin reign in your mortal body" (Rom. 6:11-12). But *in* Him we may be baptized and washed clean by His streams of mercy (I Cor. 6:11).

So, how shall we remain *in* Christ? First, we remain in Christ by *continually confessing our sins to God and seeking Jesus' righteousness* (1 John 1:9). "Come near to God and he will come near to you. Wash your hands, you sinners, and purify your hearts, you double-minded" (James 4:8). Praise God that on the cross Jesus took upon himself all the guilt and punishment for our sins! As we seek to live holy lives for Him until we are made perfect in heaven, we come to the cross daily, laying down our bad choices and being washed again and again in His blood. "Repent, then, and turn to God, so that your sins may be wiped out, that times of refreshing may come from the Lord" (Acts 3:19). Secondly, we remain in Christ by *remaining in the Word.* Jesus said, "I am in my Father, and **you are in me, and I am in you.** Whoever has my commands and keeps them is the one who loves me" (John 14:20-21a). "For no matter how many promises God has made, they are 'Yes' **in Christ Jesus**" (2 Cor. 1:20). The Bible helps us intimately know who Christ is. Thirdly, we remain in Christ as we *pray continually.* Each morning we may thank God for a new day and receive the day's agenda. During the day, we may listen for the Spirit's guidance about where and how to plant seeds of blessing. At the end of the day, we may debrief with God, seeking His forgiving grace and resting well. In all our good and bad circumstances we rejoice and give thanks because "this is God's will for you **in Christ Jesus**" (I Thess. 5:16-18). Further, we admit our sins to each other and pray together about them (James 5:16) so that we may be more Christ-like. Fourthly, we remain in Christ as we *feast at His table*, remembering and celebrating that Jesus' body and blood reset the covenant, clothing us with His righteousness and refreshing us with His Spirit. Finally, we remain in Christ as we *gather with His Church* for worship, teaching, fellowship, and prayer. We help each other walk in His footsteps and accomplish His mission.

It is crucial for us to be in Christ, but we can't live lives of meaningful purpose until we also realize that He is *in us*, pouring through us to bless the world. Grace and love are meant to be shared; they exist like flowing streams, not stagnating pools. Paul said, "offer every part of yourself to him as an *instrument* of righteousness" (Rom 6:13); "for we are God's handiwork, created in Christ Jesus *to do good works*, which God prepared in advance for us to do" (Eph. 2:10). Filled with His Spirit's power we become vessels for sharing His goodness. Sponges weren't made merely to float around! They were made to be partnering tools. Pick up a water-saturated sponge and water will drip from it, ready to be transported to where it is needed. Jesus, the Living

Water, purifies us, and then calls us to work with the Trinity in restoring the world. Their love flows through us as we carry on the mission given to Jesus by the Father. This mission is recorded in the Old Testament (Is. 61: 1-2) and claimed by Jesus in the New (Luke 4:18-19):

> "The Spirit of the Lord is on me,
>   because he has anointed me
>   to proclaim good news to the poor.
> He has sent me to proclaim freedom for the prisoners
>   and recovery of sight for the blind,
> to set the oppressed free,
>   to proclaim the year of the Lord's favor."

In accomplishing this great mission, it is comforting to know that we are not working as the Lone Sponge. We are part of Christ's baptized Church, "devoted . . . to the apostles' teaching and to fellowship, to the breaking of bread and to prayer" (Acts 2:42). "Let us consider how we may spur one another on toward love and good deeds . . . encouraging one another—and all the more as you see the Day approaching" (Heb. 10: 24-25).

Kingdom clean-up is challenging work. At any given time we may be tempted to stop because we are ignorant of the world's filth or neglectful of it or overwhelmed by it. We may be made timid by our fears of soaking up evil and faithless ideas. Yet God assures believers that "the one who is **in** you is greater than the one who is in the world" (1 John 4:4b).

Spending time in prayer with the One Who is in us is essential for accomplishing the Kingdom's mission:

> You did not choose me, but I chose you and appointed you so that you might go and bear fruit—fruit that will last—and so that whatever you ask **in my name** the Father will give you. This is my command: Love each other.
>
> (John 15:16-17)

JESUS' NAME

From the time I was a child, I ended prayers by saying, "in Jesus' name, amen." I thought that phrase was like the lisped "That's all, folks!" that Bugs Bunny always said at the end of cartoon time. "In Jesus' name" was simply my way of signing off on prayer time; it meant, "I'm done praying, God."

However, the Apostle Paul reminds us that Jesus' name is much more than a sign-off phrase: "whatever you do, whether in word or deed, **do it all in the name of the Lord Jesus**, giving thanks to God the Father through him" (Col. 3:17). Believers operate in and under the name of Jesus Christ. So, having considered the preposition *in*, let's now consider the rest of the phrase—*Jesus' name*.

An online search for the phrase "in the name of Jesus" produces many verses about *teaching* in his name, *having faith* in his name, being *healed* in his name, being *baptized* in his name, *commanding demons* in his name, being *justified* in his name, *calling on* his name, and *giving thanks* in his name. Clearly Jesus' name is important!

In the Bible, people were often seeking to know who Jesus was and they recognized him using many names. John the Baptist recognized Jesus as the "Lamb of God" (John 1:29, 36). Both at Jesus' baptism and the Transfiguration, Father called out the key: "You are my Son, whom I love; with you I am well-pleased" (Mk. 1:11; 9:7), but the evil one pretended not to get that message, tempting Jesus with "*If* you are the Son of God . . ." (Mt. 4:3). King Herod's paranoia and guilt had him thinking Jesus was the dead John the Baptist (Mt. 14:1-2). As Jesus healed people, raised the dead, and cast out demons, the Spirit opened hearts to address Jesus correctly: "the Holy One of God," "Son of God," "Son of the Most High God," "Son of David," "Son of Man." However, Jesus was not yet ready to reveal his identity, so he told these people to be quiet. Even Jesus' disciples wondered about his identity, asking in amazement and fear in their boat after Jesus calmed the storm, "Who is this?" (Mk. 4:41). They ventured the true answer after Jesus walked on water: "You are the Son of God" (Mt. 14:33), but it wasn't until the gospel plot was coming to an end, that Jesus asked Peter the two key questions in Mark 8:27-30: "Who do people say that I am?" and "Who do you say that I am?" Peter responded that people were guessing Jesus might be "John the Baptist," "Elijah," or "one of the prophets," but he believed Jesus to be the "Messiah." Then, at the crucifixion, Pontius Pilate nailed his answer to the cross: "King of the Jews" (Luke 23:3,38), even while the crowds and soldiers standing around the cross sneered, "If he is God's Messiah, the Chosen One . . . If you are the king of the Jews . . ." (Luke 23:35, 37). But when the earth shook, the sky was darkened, and the curtain of the Temple was ripped in two, the centurion announced the truth exactly: "Surely this man was the Son of God!" (Mk 15:39).

So many names and titles! Why then is the name *Jesus* so special? It is a name that has been given to many men, yet it seems to have become noteworthy only in relation to the Jesus of the Bible. Many songs have been written praising his name. Why?

It is important to remember that Jesus' name was *given to him by His Father.* When Father sent an angel to encourage Joseph to marry pregnant Mary yet refrain from sexual relations with her until the baby was born, Father also provided Joseph with the baby's name: "What is conceived in her is from the Holy Spirit. She will give birth to a son, and you are to give him the name Jesus, because he will save his people from their sins" (Mt. 1:20-21).

Just as great meaning was carried by the little word *in,* so the syllables that make up Jesus' name also carry enormous meaning. One syllable comes from the name of Father. We all know parents who have taken a syllable from one of their names and added it to the name they have given their child. (For example, my brother's name was *Aldrich*, a combination of syllables from his grandfather's name and our father's name, *Richard*.) That's what God the Father did; He lifted the syllable *yah* from His name *Yahveh. Yah* means *I AM.* To that, Father added a form of the Hebrew verb that means *to save.* Together (with changed spelling), these two syllables create the name *Yeshua—Jesus—*which means, *I AM of salvation.* Father wasn't being clever; He was reminding the world of His power flowing through His Son. *I AM* controls the biblical record. *I AM* controls history!

In Exodus, Moses pleaded with God to reveal His name, because the Israelites wanted to claim God by name as they traveled through the lands where people worshipped idol gods. God's answer to Moses was profound:

> God said to Moses, "**I AM WHO I AM**. This is what you are to say to the Israelites: '**I AM** has sent me to you . . . . **The LORD**, the God of your fathers—the God of Abraham, the God of Isaac and the God of Jacob—has sent me to you.'
>
> This is my name forever,
> the name you shall call me
> from generation to generation."
>
> (Ex. 3:14-15)

When I write "I am a woman. I am old." that verb *am* is functioning as a verb of *being*, a *linking* verb—linking the subject with information that describes or renames the subject. In a sense, this information limits the subject ("I am a woman...not a man; I am old...not young"). The verb *am* is also *present* tense—the truth expressed is here and now. Delightfully, God chooses this construction for His name, but He doesn't finish the sentence to limit Himself! *I AM* reveals Him to be unbounded, ultimate, and an eternally present Actor—a complete circle of Being, creating all, knowing all, supreme over all, in control of all, eternally alive, everywhere present, holy and set apart, yet encompassing all that exists, all powerful, only good, only true, and only beautiful—*I AM Who I AM.*

The book of Exodus was written in Hebrew. In Hebrew, the shortened form of the Hebrew words meaning *I AM WHO I AM* is *Yahveh*, but the Hebrew people refrain from speaking that Name because He is holy. Reverence for God's Name also causes them to spell *Yahveh* with only consonants, *Y-H-V-H*. The name *Yahveh* doesn't appear in our English Bibles but the introduction to my New International Version Bible explains that what does appear over 6800 times is the English substitute for *Yahveh*—*LORD*—spelled with small capital letters.

I AM or *LORD* is God's *covenant* name. He protected it within His Ten Commandments law, saying, "You shall not misuse the **name of the** LORD your God, for the LORD will not hold anyone guiltless who misuses his name" (Ex. 20:7). When Father sent prophets to call His people back into obedient covenant living, He proclaimed: "**I am the** LORD; that is my name! I will not yield my glory to another or my praise to idols" (Isaiah 42:8).

> "Let not the wise boast of their wisdom
>   or the strong boast of their strength
>   or the rich boast of their riches,
> but let the one who boasts boast about this:
>   that they have the understanding to know me,
> that **I am the** LORD, who exercises kindness,
>   justice and righteousness on earth,
>   for in these I delight."
> (Jer. 9:23-24)

> I will give them a heart to know me, that **I am the** LORD. They will be my people, and I will be their God, for they will return to me with all their heart.
> (Jer. 24:7)

> I will show the holiness of my great name, which has been profaned among the nations, the name you have profaned among them. Then the nations will know that **I am the** LORD ... when I am proved holy through you before their eyes.
> (Ez. 36:23)

Knowing he carried His Father's name, perhaps Jesus' tone was playful when he asked Peter, "Who do you say that *I am*?" because it seems the answer was in the question! Yes, Jesus is the exact representation of the Father. Even though He had the role of Son, Jesus always claimed His oneness with the Father: "I and the Father **are one**" (John 10:30).

> Very truly I tell you, the Son can do nothing by himself; he can do only what he sees his Father doing, because **whatever the Father does the Son also does.**
>
> (John 5:19)

> For I have come down from heaven not to do my will but **to do the will of him who sent me.** And this is the will of him who sent me—that I shall lose none of all those he has given me, but raise them up at the last day. For my Father's will is that everyone who looks to the Son and believes in him shall have eternal life.
>
> (John 6:38-40)

> For I did not speak on my own; but the Father who sent me, **commanded me to say all that I have spoken.**
>
> (John 12:49)

In His unity with the Father and because Jesus spoke what the Father commanded him to speak, what Jesus teaches about his name *expands* our understanding of Father and Son in at least eight ways, which I will only begin to unpack:

> **I AM—the bread of life** (John 6:35-51). He is the God of perfect, abundant, and miraculous provision. He provided manna for forty years in the wilderness and fed thousands using just a few loaves and fish.

I AM—the light of the world (John 8:12). He is the God Whose light cannot be overpowered by the darkness of evil. He created the sun, the moon, and the stars. He called us from darkness into light (1 Pet. 2:9). He radiates unimaginable light (Rev. 1:16; 21:23).

I AM—the gate (John 10:7-9). He is the God Who lies down across the sheepfold entrance to protect the lives of the sheep, even if it means being bloodied by robbers. He also welcomes us into Father's house where He is preparing rooms for us (John 14:3).

I AM—the good shepherd (John 10:11-14). He is the God Who searches for the lost sheep, carries them in His arms, and leads them into green pastures (Ps. 23). We sheep know His voice to follow Him, and He knows us (John 10:27).

I AM—the resurrection and the life (John 11:25). He is the God Who conquered death. He lives with the Father in the eternal and perfect dimension of heaven. When we submit to Him, His Spirit of resurrection life comes to live within us (Acts 2:38). We are raised to live new life in Him *now* (Acts 3:6, 16), praying and working for things to be "on earth as it is in heaven" (Mt. 6:10).

I AM—the Alpha and the Omega "who is, and was, and is to come" (Rev 1:8). He is the God Who existed before creation, chose us to be His children before creation (Eph. 1:4-6), controls and rules everything in history, and will unite heaven and earth into His perfect Kingdom (Rev. 21:1-6). Past, present, and future find their true meaning in Him. We will live eternally with Him.

I AM—the way, the truth, the life (John 14:6). He is the God Who goes ahead of each of us on our life's journey, leading us along trustworthy and true ways. He sends angels to guide and guard us (Ex. 23:20-23). He sends His Spirit to lead us into Kingdom living.

I AM—the true vine (John 15:1-5). He is the God through Whom all good efforts reach fruition. He sends His Spirit to help us produce love, joy, peace, patience, kindness, goodness, faithfulness, gentleness, and self-control (Gal 5:22-23). Through our testimonies of His life, His Church enlarges.

Father also enlarged on His *I AM* name when He gave Moses details of His wondrous loving nature. These characteristics are so essential and precious that the Bible writers recall them at least eight times (Num. 14:18; Neh. 9:17; Ps. 86:15; Ps. 103:8; Ps. 145:8-9; Joel 2:13; Jon. 4:2; Nah. 1:3). Because our LORD Jesus is one with Father, He shares this loving and just nature:

> Then the LORD came down . . . proclaiming, "The LORD, the LORD, the **compassionate and gracious God, slow to anger, abounding in love and faithfulness, maintaining love to thousands, and forgiving wickedness, rebellion and sin.** Yet he does not leave the guilty unpunished; **he punishes** the children and their children for the sin of the parents to the third and fourth generation.
>
> (Ex. 34:5-7)

As believers, we may boldly pray to Father and Son, asking Them to pour out Their compassion, grace, mercy, forgiveness, justice, abounding love, and faithfulness into our world. Further, as Christ's Body who are being transformed by the Spirit to become like Jesus Christ and are labeled with His name *Christian,* we may also humbly pray that *we* will share God's compassion, grace, mercy, forgiveness, justice, abounding love, and faithfulness with the world for the glory of His name (Ps. 115:1).

Clearly, praying in Jesus' name is not a signing off, but a signing on to the source of our salvation and to the mission and powers of heaven! This LORD is our Creator, Provider, Guide, Savior, Bridegroom, Friend and Judge. He will reward those who reverence His name (Rev. 11:18).

Although praying is as easy as talking, praying is also the profound protocol for partnering with God. When we pray in Jesus' name, our faith claims the *merits of his person*—His divine authority as God's Son, His perfect obedience and righteousness, His covenant-keeping death for our salvation. Acts 4:12 tells us, "Salvation is found in no one else, for there is no other name under heaven given to mankind by which we must be saved." When we pray in Jesus' name, we claim to *belong to the family of God,* desiring holiness, doing the will of Father, becoming adopted brothers and sisters of Jesus (Heb. 2:11; Rom. 8:29; Mk. 3:34-35) eager to pray boldly to our *Abba* and to help each other. When we pray in Jesus' name, we want to *reflect our Father* (Eph 3:14-19), seeking the Spirit's help to become children characterized by His fruit. When we pray in Jesus' name, we accept our *commissioning for Kingdom work,* pledging to carry out Father's mission, trusting in the power of His authority (Ps. 9:10; 20:7).

Also, when we pray in Jesus' name, we recognize that *life will involve suffering* (Mark 13:7-13). Jesus' suffering was intense and ongoing—He left Glory, was tempted by the devil, was harassed by the religious leaders, was misunderstood by his family and followers, was brought to tears over unbelief, grieved the deaths of friends and father, was abandoned by the disciples, and ultimately, was forsaken by Father. Yet Jesus followed his mission to the cross, wrestling in prayer in the garden of Gethsemane: "Now my soul is troubled, and what shall I say? 'Father, save me from this hour?' No, it was for this very reason I came to this hour. 'Father, *glorify your name!*'" (John 12:27).

> Therefore God exalted him to the highest place /
> and gave him **the name that is above every name,**
> **/ that at the name of Jesus** every knee should bow,
> / in heaven, and on earth, and under the earth, / and
> every tongue acknowledge that Jesus Christ is Lord,
> to the glory of God the Father.
>
> (Phil 2:9-11)

Before and since that time, Father, King Jesus, and the Spirit continue to stop the infiltrations of the evil one and bind up the world's horrendous brokenness. Working alongside Them, we can expect to suffer and to grapple in prayer for release from evil. Perhaps we will be begging for freedom from failure, or seeking the Spirit's filling as we struggle in weakness and fear. Perhaps we will be pleading for wisdom, strength, and rescue while battling the devil's many D's such as deception, divisions, dishonor, disabilities, disease, destruction, and death. Certainly we will be questioning and lamenting—our prayers will be filled with bitter weeping, weary pleading, righteous arguing, and penitent whimpering. The good news is that Father hears all these prayers and has the power to change things. Only in Him can we find grace and mercy, restoration and shalom. Such relief, given in His wisdom and His good timing, may happen slowly or never be realized this side of heaven. It will not be easy to wait. It is not be easy to go through sorrows unto death. Yet we are called to cling to Him and trust His good purposes even when we do not readily see good outcomes (Mt. 11:28-30). May our day by day conversations with God bring us the strength and hope of which Lamentations 3:22-26 assures us:

> Because of the LORD's great love we are not consumed,
>   for his compassions never fail.
> They are new every morning;
>   great is your faithfulness.
> I say to myself, "The LORD is my portion;
>   therefore I will wait for him."

The LORD is good to those whose hope is in him,
   to the one who seeks him;
it is good to wait quietly
   for the salvation of the LORD.

Until Father's deliverance happens, we are urged to stay strong and prepare for battle by studying the tactics of the enemy (1 Pet. 5:8), putting on the armor of God (Eph. 6:13-17), preparing our testimonies (1 Pet. 3:15), and listening for the Spirit's direction (John 16:13, Mark 13:11). His Spirit will empower and direct us, individually and together, into battlefields great and small. Not all battlefields will be bloody, but all battles are important. May we listen and obey as He urges our hearts to phone, write, mail, comment on social media, listen, discuss, open our homes, drive, teach, worship, testify, share our muscle, share our skills, share our resources, donate, protest, advocate, legislate, or intervene. May we always bathe our actions in prayer (Rom 8:26).

> With this in mind, we constantly pray for you, that our God may make you worthy of his calling, and that by his power he may bring to fruition your every desire for goodness and your every deed prompted by faith. We pray this so that **the name of our Lord Jesus** may be glorified **in** you and you **in** him, according to the grace of our God and the Lord Jesus Christ.
>
> (2 Thess. 1: 11-12)

Kingdom work may lead to death—it has for many believers—even so, we find our hope in Jesus. When he was about to die on the cross (Luke 23:46), Jesus surrendered his spirit to Father until he was raised to new life. Our spirits, too, will be held by Father until the resurrection day. Hallelujah (which means, *praise I AM*)!

Father promises us the power of His name. He protected the traveling Israelites by putting His name on them, commanding the

Levite priests to continually bless the people in His name, using these words with which pastors still bless their congregants today:

The **LORD** bless you
　　and keep you;
the **LORD** make his face shine on you
　　and be gracious to you;
the **LORD** turn his face toward you
　　and give you peace.

(Numbers 6:24-27)

　　Jesus petitioned the Father for this protection for his disciples and for us: "Holy Father, protect them by **the power of your name,** the name you gave me, so that they may be one as we are one" (John 17:11). When Christ comes again, believers "will see his face, and **his name** will be on their foreheads" (Rev. 22:4).

　　In His name, we are one with the Church of all ages. Throughout the Old Testament, God called men to their various roles—the *patriarchs* Abraham and Jacob, the *prophets* Moses and Isaiah, the *priest* Samuel, and David the *king*. Each responded to God's call using the same words: "Here I am!" (Gen. 22:1,11; Gen. 31:11; 46:2; Ex. 3:4; I Sam. 3:4; Ps. 40:7; Is. 6:8). The Bible goes on to record their various conversations with God about their work and His will, their troubles and His rescue, their confessed sins and His forgiveness, their self-doubts and His abundant love. May we be encouraged by those prayerful conversations and may we find a model in their "Here I am." May we stand with raised hands before the LORD to pray:

Here, I AM!
Here I am!
Use me to glorify Your Name in all the earth!
In Jesus' Name,
Amen.

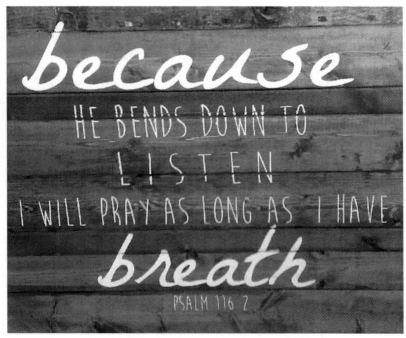

Wall hanging quoting Psalm 116:2 (NLT)

BREATHING WITH THE BREATH

When I was a child, churches referred to the Spirit as "the Holy Ghost," a rather scary name! How would a child imagine such a Person? As I grew older, I learned that the Spirit is equal to Jesus and the Father, but invisible. He never speaks on His own. He is present everywhere, yet He lives in our hearts. He can be "resisted" by hard-hearted hearers of Jesus' truth (Acts 7:51, *NIV*) who are warned not to "quench" Him (I Thess. 5:19) nor to "grieve" Him (Eph. 4:30). Yet the Spirit is directed by God to soften our hearts and to produce faith in us (it is a gift, not a work), so that we become the joyful recipients of His "irresistible grace." Who is this Person?

The Athanasian Creed and the Nicene Creed both teach that the Spirit, though not created, originates and flows from the Father and the Son. In his *Daily Gospel Reflections* (https://wordonfire. org, July 15, Aug. 14, 2020), Bishop Robert Barron describes the Person of the Holy Spirit as the *love* that emanates from the Father and the Son as They continually communicate. I resonate with such descriptions, even though they bring to mind a fluidity I can't imagine in a Person. Nevertheless, the concept of the breathing Spirit is echoed throughout the Bible.

BREATH, WIND, SPIRIT

I delight in the Bible's metaphors, similes, parables, symbols, names, puns and word-play. In relation to the Spirit, scholars point out that in the biblical texts, the Hebrew word *ruach* and the Greek word *pneuma* can interchangeably mean *breath, wind,* and *Spirit.* Notice how those words dance together in the passages that follow (emphasis forward, mine).

The Bible describes the intimate, face-to-face, mouth to nostrils way that people came into existence: "Then the LORD God formed a man from the dust of the ground and **breathed** into his nostrils the **breath of life,** and the man became a living being" (Gen. 2:7). Besides the blessing of being alive, what might our breath signify? In his

Nooma video titled *Breathe* (Zondervan), Pastor Rob Bell notes that voicing the Hebrew consonants of God's name YHWH—*Yod-heh-vav-heh*—echoes the sound of breathing. Stop a moment and try it: Breathe in saying *Yod*, breathe out saying *heh*, breathe in on *vav*, and breathe out on *heh*. Pastor Bell suggests that from our first baby breath to our final dying gasp, our breathing may be "voicing" the name of the LORD. I am intrigued by this idea, by the belonging and intimacy our breath might carry. I wonder if, perhaps, we are "tagged" with God as our Owner through our breathing, or if, perhaps, our breathing is itself a prayer, unceasingly calling on the name of the LORD.

After rebelling against God, sinful humans chose to worship idols who had "**no breath** in them" (Jer. 10:14, Hab. 2:19). So God sent His people into the time-out of captivity to reconsider their choices. During that time, the prophet Ezekiel was told to share with the Israelites the vision of the Valley of Dry Bones (Ez. 37:1-14). In that vision, God directed him to command a field of bones to come to life. Ezekiel did so, and the bones rattled together into an army of skeletons upon which flesh appeared, but there was no *life* in them. Then the LORD said:

> Prophesy to **the breath**; prophesy, son of man, and say to it, "This is what the Sovereign LORD says: 'Come, breath, from the four **winds** and **breathe** into these slain, that they may live.'" So I prophesied as he commanded me, and **breath** entered them; they came to life and stood up on their feet . . . . This is what the Sovereign LORD says: "My people, I am going to open your graves and bring you up from them; I will bring you back to the land of Israel. Then you, my people, will know that I am the LORD . . . . I will put my **Spirit** in you and you will live . . . ."
>
> (Ez. 37: 9-10, 12, 14a)

Hundreds of years later, using similar imagery, Jesus taught Nicodemus:

Very truly I tell you, no one can enter the kingdom of God unless they are born of water and the Spirit. Flesh gives birth to flesh, but **the Spirit** gives birth to **spirit** . . . The **wind** blows wherever it pleases. You hear its sound, but you cannot tell where it comes from or where it is going. So it is with everyone born of the **Spirit**.

(John 3:5-6, 8)

Before he returned to Glory, in a precious echo of God's intimate creation of man, Jesus "kissed" his disciples giving them the gift of new life in the Spirit: " 'As the Father has sent me, I am sending you.' And with that he **breathed** on them and said, 'Receive the **Holy Spirit**'" (John 20:21-22). Then he ascended into heaven, and from there blessed *all* believers with the gift of the Holy Spirit on Pentecost (Acts 2:2-4). The **Spirit** arrived with the sound of a violent **wind** and with what seemed to be tongues of fire. All believers were moved to testify. Years later, writing to the Christians in Rome, the Apostle Paul taught powerfully about living the resurrection life of the Spirit: "[We] do not live according to the flesh but according to the **Spirit**...and by him we cry 'Abba, Father.' The Spirit himself testifies with our **spirit** that we are God's children" (Rom. 8:4b, 15b-16).

To his disciples and to us, Jesus promised that "the **Holy Spirit**, whom the Father will send in my name, will teach you all things and will remind you of everything I have said to you" (John 14:26). Many of the things Jesus said are contained in the *Spirit-inspired* Word: "All Scripture is **God-breathed** and is useful for teaching, rebuking, correcting and training in righteousness so that the man of God may be thoroughly equipped for every good work" (2 Tim. 3:16). The Spirit never speaks His own thoughts (John 16:13), but points us to the Word, so when I open my Bible after praying for the Spirit's guidance, I imagine that the pages "exhale" with the Spirit's living breath, echoing the conversations of the Trinity. In that regard, I often sing and pray Hatch's 1878 hymn:

Breathe on me, Breath of God,
Fill me with life anew,
That I may love the way you love,
And do what you would do.
(https://hymnary.org/text/breathe_on_me_breath_of_god)

SEVEN-FOLD SPIRIT

Our pastor often ends worship services using the blessing found in Rev. 1:4-5:

Grace and peace to you from him who is, and who was, and who is to come, **and from the seven spirits before his throne**, and from Jesus Christ, who is the faithful witness, the firstborn from the dead, and the ruler of the kings of the earth.

That blessing and other references to the *seven spirits* or *seven-fold Spirit* (Rev. 3:1; 4:5; 5:6) are an example of how numbers hold deeper meanings to the writers of the Bible. The number seven symbolizes "wholeness and completeness," so the seven-fold Spirit is the Holy Spirit in His fullness, in the completeness of His role, in the wholeness of all His attributes. He likely has many more attributes than seven, but Isaiah 11:2-3 mentions these attributes when describing the coming of Jesus:

The Spirit of the Lord will rest on him—
the Spirit of **wisdom** and of **understanding,**
the Spirit of **counsel** and of **might,**
the Spirit of the **knowledge** and **fear of the**
Lord and he will delight in the fear of the Lord.

These attributes echo the imaginative poetry of Proverbs 8, where wisdom is personified as a woman. Lady Wisdom offers believers similar blessings: wisdom, knowledge, counsel, the fear of the Lord, understanding, power, and discernment/prudence. Wisdom also promises: "Blessed are those who listen to me, / watching daily at my doors, / waiting at my doorway. / For those who find me find life / and receive favor from the LORD" (Prov. 8:34-35).

Truly, the Holy Spirit brings wisdom, pointing us to Father's truth and to Jesus' teachings. How blessed we are that God is willing to occupy our brains as well as our hearts! In a world that thrives on lies and evil, we are privileged to have daily access to God's wisdom in His Word and to pray for the Spirit's leading and light when testing the spirits (I John 4:1-6). He enables us to become wise and discerning believers, thus reflecting the Trinity.

MORE PICTURES OF THE SPIRIT

The Bible's imagery of the Spirit is rich beyond measure. I want to glorify His name by briefly referencing several other Spirit analogies that readers may wish to explore in the Word and address in their prayers.

The Spirit is like a *Sower of Seed.* He impregnated Mary with Jesus, whom Galatians 3:16-19 calls "the Seed." He also scatters the seed of the Word (Jesus) into the soil of our hearts (I Pet. 1:23). As we nurture that Word, the Spirit develops in us Christ-likeness and fruitfulness—love, joy, peace, patience, kindness, goodness, faithfulness, gentleness, and self-control (Gal. 5:22-23).

The Spirit is like a *Master Teacher.* He inspired the Bible's authors and brings to our minds the exact parts of Father's Word that we need for our instruction at any given moment. He brings to our minds verses that develop love and trust, that cause us to repent and seek forgiveness, that warn us, that energize and enable us for ministry, that raise our hopes, that lift us into worship. He is the ultimate tutor of our faith.

The Spirit is like *Christ's Body Builder*, calling the Church to faith and to the work of Christ (I Cor. 12). He helps us become like Jesus (Eph 4). He connects us together in love, urges us to forgive, and strengthens us to serve. He stretches us to pray for each other and lifts us up to receive God's mercy and grace. He makes the church strong and bold.

Therefore, since we have such a hope, we are very bold. We are not like Moses, who would put a veil over his face . . . . But whenever anyone turns to the Lord, the veil is taken away. Now the Lord is the Spirit, and where the Spirit of the Lord is, there is freedom. And we all, who with unveiled faces contemplate the Lord's glory, are being transformed into his image with ever-increasing glory, which comes from the Lord, who is the Spirit.

(2 Cor. 3: 12-13,16-18)

The Spirit is like *God's Communications Director*, guiding both heaven's revelation and human's response. He inspired the writing of the Word. He also guards and guides Father's Truth into the world, inspiring pastors, teachers, authors, song writers, artists, and all believers to testify about God. The Spirit opens hearts so that the Word on the page transforms our lives. The Spirit helps us see the presence of God in our lives (Eph 1:17-19). Further, the Spirit calls forth our praise, worship, and prayer. (Most worship songs are prayers and wonderful ways to engage with the Trinity.) He convicts us to live out Father's will and orchestrates our decisions around that conviction (Acts 16:6-7). He brings people and concerns to mind so that we pray for them. He delivers our prayers to the throne room of heaven. He even groans prayers *for us* when our hearts don't know how to proceed or what to ask (Rom. 8:26-27).

The following verse from a hymn attributed to R. Maurus and paraphrased in the 17th century by poet John Dryden, has been sung in churches since the 9th century. I encourage you to pray or sing it:

Plenteous of grace, descend from high,
rich in thy sevenfold energy;
make us eternal truths receive
and practice all that we believe;
give us thyself that we may see
the Father and the Son by thee.
(https://hymnary.org/text/creator_spirit_by_whose_aid)

TALKING WITH THE TRINITY

Whenever I speak from the Word, I ask the Spirit to bring to my mind the ideas He wants the audience to hear. I also ask Him to lead me to a visual aid that reflects the part of the Word that I will be sharing. Many of us are visual learners, so when I teach I like to use gestures or drawings, objects or a display board. Visuals help us make connections and remember concepts.

I began seriously pondering the relationship of the Persons of the Trinity in 2019 when it was my turn to bring the Word during the weekly service our church provides at a care home for the elderly. The topic that came to my mind was "the Trinity." It seemed an odd topic because younger thinkers often find it difficult to grasp the concept of the Three-in-One, so how much more challenging might that topic be for aging saints? Nevertheless, having come to trust the Spirit's urgings, I tackled it, checking the Scriptures, the creeds and confessions of my church, and various explanations on Reformed websites. When the time came, I felt sufficiently tutored and inspired to preach on "Talking with the Trinity." Thankfully, I also felt led to create the hand-drawn sketch on the preceding page, which I now find useful when talking about the Trinity.

In expanded form, this chapter contains the message from the Word that I presented at the care home using the visual. I hope that the pictures help you recall ideas from the previous three chapters and visualize their relationship. I hope this chapter will help you appreciate the privilege of prayer.

LET'S START AT THE TOP!

The top triangle probably seems familiar (yet different), because an equilateral triangle is commonly used to represent the three persons of the Trinity—Father, Son, and Holy Spirit—of one essence, yet distinct and equal. We usually place the Father at the peak of the triangle because His will directs and sustains all things; we assign the bottom corners to the Son and the Spirit. I have inverted the triangle, however, to remind us that the Father has enthroned the resurrected Son at His right hand. Further, if we fold the triangle in half from top to bottom, the halves "mirror" each other, illustrating that the Son is "the exact representation" of the Father. Hebrews 1:3-4 teaches this (emphasis forward, mine):

> The Son is the radiance of God's glory and **the exact representation of his being**, sustaining all things by his powerful word. After he had provided purification for sins, he sat down **at the right hand of the Majesty** in heaven. So he became as much superior to the angels as the name he has inherited is superior to theirs.

What energizes this portion of the visual is that the Spirit's angle points down, showing that He flows into our world. He breathes life into all creation. He pours Father's truth into our world. He was sent to reside in our hearts as Teacher. He also "megaphones" our prayers back to Jesus and Father.

Father, Son, and Spirit—Three-in-One! Stop a moment and use your Biblical imagination to ponder the eternal bustle and inter-relatedness of the Trinity, as they move around in their unity, working together, planning how they will create and love the world. The Bible points to their unified yet shared activity—the Father setting forth His loving purposes, the Son obediently acting to carry out the plans, and the Spirit hovering to breathe definition into the universe, nurture seeds, and give life to all creatures (Gen. 1:1, John 1:1-3).

In the visual, another triangle "mirrors" the Trinity triangle to illustrate that all humankind on earth were made in the image of God. Genesis records some of the Trinity's discussion about that: "Then God said, "Let us make mankind **in our image**, in **our likeness**, so that they may rule over the fish in the sea and the birds in the sky, over the livestock and all the wild animals, and over all the creatures that move along the ground" (Gen. 1: 26). What a grand design! The "earth triangle" also points *up* to show that humans can approach and communicate with the Trinity. During those first days of perfection in Eden, Adam and Eve walked and talked with God. It was a glorious life of interaction. They participated with the Trinity in love, talking with God and tending His garden. As God's image-bearers, they also mirrored the Trinity in their human relationships, working together for a unified purpose and sharing loving communication. If that had been the end of the story, nothing more would need to be illustrated.

Sadly, the wicked fallen angel, the devil (who was already at war with Father), showed up and rebelliously lied to Adam and Eve, suggesting that God did *not* want them to image Him. He planted seeds of selfish arrogance, suggesting that they should know *everything* that God knew—including God's knowledge of evil (Gen. 3:5). Foolishly, Adam and Eve neglected to discuss the devil's temptation with God. Instead, they turned to breathe in his toxic vapor of evil. Only God's grace saved them; God banished them from the Garden to protect them from eating of the tree of eternal life and living eternally with evil (Gen. 3:21-28), but ever after their Fall into sin, all humans are prone to choose evil and suffer its consequences (Rom. 5:12). The evil became so overwhelming, that God chose to destroy the people and cleanse the earth with the Flood, saving only believing Noah and his family. However, the generations after Noah also sinned and when they chose to build a tower to heaven, God scattered them over the earth.

Seeking a faithful patriarch to build a chosen people, God entered into covenant with Abraham and his descendants to be their God and shape them into a people who would testify to His glory throughout the world. Abraham's grandson Jacob (Israel) had twelve sons and they became a great nation. Sadly, they, too, disobeyed God and turned to idols. For their own growth and good, God allowed them to be enslaved in Egypt for hundreds of years.

Then, when the time was right, God called Moses to free them and lead them into the Promised Land (Ex. 3). Though afraid of public speaking, thankfully, Moses was not afraid to talk to God. His pleas for God's presence to abide with the Israelites demonstrate the confidence with which believers can pray to God. In fact, Moses kept such close prayerful contact with God, that his face mirrored God's glory, shining so brightly that he had to veil his face in the presence of the people (Ex. 34:29-35).

ENTER GOD'S WRITTEN WORD!

God knew that His precious children were prone to wander, so to point them back to Him, He gifted them with boundaries. These guidelines showed them and show us how to live with Him, with each other, and with the creation. He wrote this Law on tablets of stone with His own finger. That Law and others are found in the first five books of our Bible. Later, the Spirit inspired other authors to write down more of God's truth, creating the full Bible. This same Spirit calls us to receive those God-breathed words. He is willing to enter into open hearts and capture open minds, so that we may hear God's voice in the Bible and affirm with Moses, "They are not just idle words for you—they are your life" (Deut. 32:47).

Hundreds of years passed. The Israelites were led by judges, ruled by kings, destroyed by invaders, and taken captive only to return in Father's grace and rebuild. Through it all, they continued to test God and often wandered.

ENTER THE SON!

When the time was right, Father sent His Son to earth to save the misguided and sinful people He still loved. The precious Son "gave up His glory" (Phil. 2:6-8) to become the Son of Man. Working in trinity, the Holy Spirit implanted Father's Seed into Mary's womb (Luke 1:35), and the Son was born a baby, the infant Jesus.

> In the beginning was the Word, and the Word was with God, and the Word was God . . . . The Word became flesh and made his dwelling among us. We have seen his glory, the glory of the one and only Son, who came from the Father, full of grace and truth. (John 1:1-2, 14)

Jesus lived on earth for thirty-three years, growing up and experiencing all of our human ways and sufferings. He was willing to set aside his *dependence* on his divine powers to live a fully human life. During the final three years of his earthly life, Jesus both taught and demonstrated how the Trinity's divine love and power can be realized within redeemed human beings. His bloody death as the final sacrificial Lamb fulfilled the old covenant with Abraham, saved us to be God's people, and sealed our new covenant with God in Christ's blood, opening the door to the glories of heaven. Rising and ascending, Jesus fully manifested God's victorious power over the evil one, sin, and death. Therefore, in the visual, the cross stands at the apex of the human triangle.

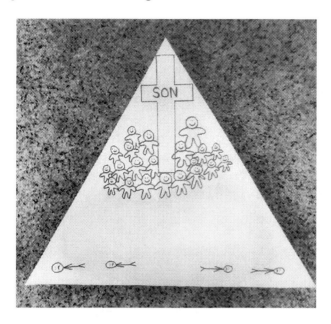

People are pictured clustered around the cross to show that, as we repent of our sins and call on God's name, Christ's death and resurrection save us and change us. In gratitude, we take up our crosses and follow Him. Through His Spirit we live the new life of His already-but-not-yet Kingdom, even while we await the day when we will die and be resurrected to live eternally with the Trinity (Rom. 8:9). As the Apostle Paul writes: "I have been crucified with Christ and I no longer live, but Christ lives in me. The life I now live in the body, I live by faith in the Son of God, who loved me and gave himself for me" (Gal. 2:20).

Sadly, not all people will come to stand at the cross. The Bible tells us that Father has given to Jesus those who will become believers (John 10:28-30). Others will harden their hearts. Although blessed with the earthly life which the Spirit has breathed into them, they will spurn Father's gifts of grace and eternal life. Like fruit dropped from the vine, they will come to nothing (John 15:5-8). Eternal death will be theirs. In the visual, they lie dead.

Dear reader, have you received new life in Jesus? That life can begin as soon as your repentant heart prays to God, acknowledging His choosing of you as His child:

> *Holy God, I am a sinner and I am sorry for my sins. I believe that You have forgiven me, because Jesus paid the price for me with His blood. Thank You! Please create victorious new life in me. Fill me with Your Spirit and help me turn away from every temptation and live my life for You. I want to love You and trust You. I want to learn your ways and do Your will every day. In Jesus Name, I pray. Amen.*

WELCOME THE SPIRIT!

Jesus was thirty when he left the family carpentry business. He was inducted into his time of ministry by the other Persons of the Trinity at his baptism in the Jordan River where his cousin John was preaching repentance and baptism for the forgiveness of sins. Although Jesus was sinless, he participated in that baptism washing, modeling that repentance is necessary for forgiveness. Suddenly, Father's voice spoke from heaven: "This is my Son, whom I love; with him I am well pleased" (Mt. 3:17). How these words must have reassured Jesus of his holy identity, but also confirmed to him his calling to be the perfect lamb for the final covenant sacrifice. Additionally, a dove descended as a symbol to assure Jesus that he was being sent out to minister in the full power of God's Spirit. (After Jesus' death, water baptism came to signify that believers' hearts are washed in the blood of the Lamb and are filled with the transforming presence of God's Spirit, enabling them also to obey and live as God's children with whom He is "well-pleased.")

All Spirit-filled obedient hearts desire to live for God and feel the need to pray. While on earth, Jesus used prayer to connect with Father. Jesus prayed both personally and publicly, blessing food, giving thanks, and seeking Father's power to release healing through his hands. He prayed during times of meditation and during times of enemy temptation. He prayed seeking solace at the end of exhausting days. He prayed to lift up His disciples to Father (Luke 3:21; 5:16; 6:12; 9:18; 22:32; Mt. 14:23; 14:19; 19:13; 26:36, 39, 42, 44; Mk. 1:35; 6:46). Always he prayed with a humble and submissive heart, "yet not as I will, but as you will" (Mt. 26:39).

Jesus' death and resurrection began the unification of heaven and earth. His righteousness opened the door of heaven for us and His Spirit teaches us how to draw near. It is at the juncture of the two triangles in the visual that I point out how the Spirit works, like Father's Communication Director, between heaven and earth. The Spirit hears Father's will in heaven, records Father's will in the Word, teaches our hearts to know Father's will through the Word, leads us to pray for Father's will to be done on earth as it is in heaven, and brings our prayers back to heaven. Our prayers are received in heaven where Jesus is already praying for us and Father hears them all in Jesus' name.

We can expect that praying will change us. The Trinity's goal is for us to love as They love. As we become loving and compassionate servants, our priorities and schedules will change. We will consult with the Trinity daily about the Kingdom agenda. Perhaps we will be asked to do something comfortable and kind; perhaps the agenda will involve things terrible and frightening; perhaps we will face death. Whatever the Trinity's agenda, we may trust that through the Word and the Spirit they are with us, holding us close, pointing us to Their truth and power, and hearing our prayers.

Being loved by the Trinity and loving Them back is a precious, glorious and unmatched relationship. We are called to work with Them and converse with Them anywhere, anytime, about everything! And then, on some glorious day, the trumpets will sound and They will appear. Heaven and earth (the visual's two triangles) will unite into a shared space of glorious beauty (Eph 1:10). Believers from the past and present will rise to live with the Trinity and worship God in the perfection of God's new garden (Rev. 21:3-4). Glory will shine and, like Moses' face, our faces will reflect Their glory as we walk and talk with Father, Son, and Spirit—face to face—forevermore!

ADORATION OF THE TRINITY

Our Father, whom have we in heaven but You?

You are Supreme in the universe—

> *You are so **powerful***
> *that You spoke just a word and the world came to be.*
> *You defeated the devil and command hosts of angels.*

> *You are so **righteous** and **holy***
> *that we are awed to come intoYour presence to talk with God!*

> *You are so **intelligent***
> *that after thousands of years we are just discovering a bit*
> *of what You placed into our world and into our bodies.*

> *You are so **orderly***
> *that everything we investigate has a pattern.*

> *You are so **wise** in Your timing and discipline*
> *that only with hindsight do we begin to understand.*

> *You are so **attentive***
> *that even now You hear every prayer of each person*
> *all around the world.*

> *You are so **generous***
> *that each day You give each one of us*
> *more gifts than we could list.*

> *You are so **just** that You demanded the death penalty,*
> *yet so **loving** that You sent Your only Son to die for us,*
> *and so **forgiving**,*
> *that You take us back again and again and again.*

Father, we praise You. We love You.

Talking with the Trinity

Dear Jesus, *whom should we follow but You?*

You are our perfect example...

> *of* **humility** *— living without place or possessions;*
>
> *of* **compassion** *— healing the sick, feeding thousands, comforting mourners;*
>
> *of* **respect** *— bestowing value on children and scorned women and outcasts;*
>
> *of* **power** *— raising the dead, commanding demons, withstanding Satan's temptations.*
>
> *You were so* **truthful** *that thousands gathered to hear Your masterful teaching.*
>
> *You were so* **visionary** *that twelve men left their jobs to follow You.*
>
> *You were so* **obedient**, *that spit and insults, thorns and a cross could not deter Your purpose.*
>
> *You were so* **righteous** *and* **loving** *that You accomplished the Father's will, even though it meant agonizing death.*
>
> *What a Savior you are!*
>
> *You are so* **majestic**, *ruling from Your throne at the Father's right hand, that whole hosts of angels are needed to sing Your glory!*

How we want to be like You!
How we desire to glorify Your name!

Christ Jesus, we praise You. We love You.

Holy Spirit, whom shall we desire but You?

*You are such an **intimate** God, alongside us and within us!*
Not the closest person to us can claim to know, as You do,
our inmost thoughts, or when each hair falls from our heads.

In marvelous ways You bring us to faith and freedom.

> ***Powerfully** you melt us and mold us,*
> *changing us from earthen vessels into Your temple.*
> ***Deftly**, You open our hearts and minds*
> *to understand the Bible.*
> ***Patiently**, You listen to our requests and cries,*
> *translating those pleas into prayers of beauty*
> *which fit the Father's will and move His heart.*

> *Your wise **discernment** enables us to recognize evil;*
> *Your mighty **courage** sends us out to battle the devil;*
> *Your **inspiration** moves us to witness to the truth;*
> *Your **blessing** makes our efforts succeed.*

> *In You we are **united**, in You we are **strong**.*

> *Only You give limitless **joy** and **peace**.*

> *Only You can make us **patient, kind, good, faithful, gentle**.*

> *Constantly, You **comfort** us,*

> *and so closely do You **hold** us, that nothing, not even death, can*
> *separate us from Your love.*

Holy Spirit, we praise You. We love You.

Father, Son, and Holy Spirit — Three in One,
we worship You and adore You always.

Amen.

NEVER ALONE

In the spring of 2020, the whole world entered into more than a year-long pandemic struggle with the Covid-19 virus. To stop the infections and death rates from spreading, we sheltered in our homes, sanitized shared surfaces, and wore masks in public. Businesses shut down; gatherings and graduations were cancelled; schools and churches closed. People found new and creative ways to communicate—air hugs, car parades, computer tours of attractions, online cultural events, streamed worship services, videoed conferences and virtual classrooms. Months of quarantine caused us to ache for the precious gifts of touch, talk, and togetherness.

God created our world to connect and fellowship. Our desire for community reflects His communal nature. Although He could have lived alone and acted alone, God chose to live in community; the Trinity is the eternally unified Three-in-One God, communicating together, working together, and sharing love. Amazingly, They desire humans to reflect Their loving unity, so They created us in Their image to communicate with each other, work together in the beauty of creation, and share love, too.

They also invite us into sweet communion *with* Them, to work *with* Them and to converse *with* Them. Although it may seem confusing in print, believers readily pray to the "LORD" or to "God" and speak of "Him"—as One—knowing that the Persons of God are unified in essence, purpose, and will. Believers also pray to "Father," to "Jesus," and to the "Spirit," seeking each Person's particular works even while recognizing that They work as One. This Three-in-One God provides the precious conduit of prayer whereby earth can converse with heaven—we can talk to Them and They will listen to us. Moreover, God will consider what we say so that, in addition to praising and thanking God, we may voice our requests for Their provision and Their power and may bring to God our heartfelt desires about what is going on. I believe God is willing to listen to our opinions about our world and to hear our thoughts about His gracious love, His terribly wise judgments, and His sovereign purposes. We see Him doing so in conversations with Adam, Noah, Hagar, Joshua, Elisha, Hannah, Samuel, Solomon, Daniel, John, the prophets, and others recorded in the Bible. The will of God can never be thwarted by such prayers, but because He has chosen to work out His will in some measure through human agency, I believe His ways may be discussed. He may even choose to "'change" His mind after we converse (Ex. 32:14; Jer. 26:19 Amos 7:1-6). Being led by the Spirit to study His Word to learn His will, we are privileged to discuss life with Him. Having confessed our sins, having repented, and having been washed in Jesus' blood, we may seek to righteously represent Him. I believe God enjoys working with us, shaping and empowering us through prayer to accomplish His plans (Eph 3:12).

I am reminded of conversations that happen when I tutor children. Like Father who wants His will to be done, my goal is that the child to do the lesson. The child might say, "I *want* a red stylus to work the IPAD!" Pointing her heart to polite interaction, I first rephrase her request, "*Please, may I have* a red stylus." The obedient child amends her request, parroting my words, "Please, may I have a red stylus?" At that point, I gladly give her the red stylus because she needs it to do the lesson. By means of our conversation together, my plan for the day is fulfilled, and the child's heart is (hopefully) shaped and blessed. I believe this illustrates how we are tutored and changed during our conversations with God. The Spirit convicts our hearts of God's will and points us to pray righteously. Pleased when our prayers reflect His will, God answers us with love and blessing.

The Trinity also designed prayer as a means to carry God's love across all human boundaries. Believers can petition God about people they have never met and about places around the globe they have never been and may never be allowed to be—without even moving from their chairs. What an overarching blessing such prayers are for distant friends and family, participants in global events, victims of disasters and wars, prisoners and refugees, leaders, agencies and missionaries—to be talked about with the powerful and loving God!

Through prayer, human beings are *never alone*. God is *with* us, we can be *with* each other, and we are *with* God.

GOD is WITH US

When I purchased my house years ago, I dedicated it to God. I asked Him to use it as a place where people could be welcomed, listened to, fed, and prayed over. Houses are great places in which to gather with others to experience love and security and God. Throughout the Bible, God designed various "earthly houses" to signify *He* was living *with* His people and was open to *conversing* with them. We see this in the Garden, the tent of meeting, the tabernacle, the Temple, the person of Jesus, human hearts, the Church, and the New Jerusalem.

Adam and Eve were created by God to live with Him in the **Garden** of Eden, a beautiful and precious place of care and *conversation.* However, when they fell into sin, the Creator banished His creatures and "placed . . . cherubim and a flaming sword flashing back and forth to guard the way to the tree of life" (Gen 3:24). What a loss!

Hundreds of years later, the book of Exodus describes Moses special relationship with God. They conversed together at the **tent of meeting**, among other things discussing the need for God's presence *with* His people (emphasis forward, mine):

> As Moses went into the tent, the pillar of cloud would come down and stay at the entrance, while the LORD was **with** Moses . . . The LORD would speak to Moses face to face, as one speaks to a friend . . . .
>
> Moses said to the LORD, "You have been telling me, 'Lead these people,' but you have not let me know whom you will send **with** me . . . ."
>
> The LORD replied, "**My Presence will go with you**, and I will give you rest."
>
> Then Moses said to him, "If your Presence does not go **with** us, do not send us up from here. How will anyone know that you are pleased with me and with your people unless you **go with us**? What else will distinguish me and your people from all the other people on the face of the earth?"
>
> And the LORD said to Moses, "I will do the very thing you have asked, because I am pleased with you and I know you by name."
>
> (Ex. 33: 9-17)

Keeping His promise, God designed the **tabernacle,** a mobile home and worship center, wherein the Israelites could experience His presence as they traveled and be assured that He was *with* them. He gave them very specific design plans for building it and assigned each tribe some part of the setting up, taking down, and transporting of the tent structure.

At one end was the Holy of Holies, closed off from the people's view by a curtain. In front of that curtain, God commanded that an altar of incense be built (Ex. 30:1-8). The incense offered there morning and evening signified the *continual, daily prayers* of the people; they were "conversing" with God and He was listening to them. Yearly, this prayer altar needed to be purified, using blood to cleanse any unrighteousness in the Israelites' conversations (Ex. 30:10). The Israelites were aware of God's immediate presence with them when He appeared as a cloud of smoke in the Holy of Holies. God would also signal His desire for them to settle down or be on the move by lowering or lifting His cloud. As awesome as that must have been, it was also challenging! In Exodus 40:34-38, it seems that God was teaching His people obedience by using a "cloud-and-camp" regimen—although it was an all-day job to set up the tabernacle, sometimes after just one overnight, God would lift His cloud, signaling them to tear it down and hit the road again!

Designed to be kept inside the Holy of Holies was the magnificent Ark of the Covenant—the *heart* of God's presence—overlaid with gold, covered by the gold atonement mercy seat and adorned with hammered-gold spread-winged cherubim (Ex. 25:10-22). (The design for this "vehicle" may have been another way of shaping His people's hearts, because to produce this magnificent Ark, the released-with-riches former slaves had to give up their gold for God's glory.) Of course, no box can contain the Almighty God. Nevertheless, God used the Ark to symbolize His holy presence, designing the Ark to be carried on long poles so that no man's hands would touch it, and if they did, that man would die (2 Sam. 6:6-7). God further commanded that the tablets of His law—His covenant written on stone with His finger—be placed inside the Ark. Eventually other signs of His powerful presence were added—Aaron's budding rod and a jar of manna (Heb. 9:4). God's intention was not to create a magical talisman box, but to remind them that He was always *with* them (Ps 114:1-2). God commanded that this Ark be carried by priests through flood-stage rivers thought to be under the control of Baal to show that God was sovereign and that He could safely lead the Israelites into the Promised Land (Joshua 3). He commanded that the Ark be carried around the crumbling walls of Jericho to indicate that God was defeating that city without the Israelites lifting a war weapon (Joshua 6). When the Israelites had settled in the Promised Land, and the Ark shifted from place to place, blessings fell upon the places where it was housed (2 Sam. 6:11). Finally, King David insured that it would reside in the capital city of Jerusalem (2 Sam. 15). He planned to house it in a temple he would build for God, but Father assigned that construction job to his son.

King David was often on the run or hiding from his enemies in caves. Lacking a house for God, David still chose to converse regularly with "my rock, in whom I take refuge" (Ps. 18:2). In fact, God called David "a man after my own heart" (I Sam. 13:14; cf. Acts 13:22) and David's love for God is evident in the many *prayer-songs* David wrote. Even when God seemed silent, David continued to sing and pray, asking Him to "arise," "hear my prayer," "rescue me," "deliver me," "save me." He trusted that God was *with* him, was hearing him, and would act out of love: "In the morning, LORD, you hear my voice; in the morning I lay my requests before you and wait expectantly" (Ps. 5:3). Such daily **heart-to-heart** living with God is a good model for us.

David's son Solomon eventually built the magnificent **Temple** in Jerusalem. The priests placed the Ark inside the newly curtained Holy of Holies. "The cloud filled the temple of the Lord. And the priests could not perform their service because of the cloud, for the glory of the Lord filled his temple" (1 Kings 8:10-11). After all those years of traveling and settling, God's presence was still evident *with* His people! Solomon seemed overwhelmed, praying: "But will God really dwell on earth? The heavens, even the highest heaven, cannot contain you. How much less this temple I have built" (1 Kings 8: 27)! God responded with a promise and a warning:

> "Now my eyes will be open and my ears attentive to the *prayers* offered in this place. I have chosen and consecrated this temple so that my Name may be there forever. My eyes and my heart will always be there....

"But if you turn away and forsake the decrees and commands I have given you and go off to serve other gods and worship them, then I will uproot Israel from my land, which I have given them, and will reject this temple I have consecrated for my Name."

(2 Chr. 7:15-16, 19-20a)

Sadly, God's people did forsake Him, continuing to break covenant and worship idol gods. After putting up with their bad behavior for hundreds of years, God determined that His people needed a time-out for discipline. He allowed that beautiful Temple to be destroyed and His people to be taken into exile in Babylon. Yet, even during their 70 years of captivity, He continued to be *with* them, talking to them through prophets such as Ezekiel, calling them back to covenant love and faithfulness:

This is what the Sovereign LORD says: "Although I sent them far away among the nations and scattered them among the countries, yet for a little while **I have been a sanctuary** for them in the countries where they have gone . . . . I will gather you from the nations and bring you back . . . .

(Ez. 11:16-17)

God did deliver them, and He allowed them to return to Jerusalem and rebuild the Temple prior to the time of Jesus.

Matthew's gospel opens the New Testament, repeating the prophet Isaiah's joyful promise of God's saving presence with His people, recording the words of the angel who announced to Joseph that his son was about to arrive: "The virgin will conceive and give birth to a son, and they will call him Immanuel (which means 'God with us')" (Mt. 1:23). Jesus' arrival on earth meant that God was *with* us in **Jesus**! The **body** of the Son of God—Who perfectly obeyed the Father and Who was filled with the Spirit—was the "temple of

God." His temple-body would be destroyed when men crucified him, but after three days, it would be "rebuilt" because his flesh would be resurrected (John 2:19). With Jesus on earth, the Ark and the Temple were no longer needed to access God; however, until His death and resurrection took place and until people understood Who Jesus was, Jesus continued to honor and visit the physical Temple, claiming it to be "my Father's house," learning the Scriptures there as a youth (Luke 2:46-49), and teaching there at times during his ministry (Luke 21:37). He even sought to purify His Father's house, overturning the tables of moneychangers (John 2:14-16) and claiming its key activity: "My house will be called a house of *prayer*" (Mt. 21:13; cf. Is. 56:7). I wonder how many of those people realized that they were *with* God when they were standing near to learn from Jesus, or were crying out from a storm-tossed boat to be saved, or were falling at his feet to be healed, or were receiving his touch to regain sight, or were being gathered into his arms to be cherished, or were hearing his command to be raised from the dead. Most would not have considered that their *every-day conversations* with him or their *worshipful thanks* were *prayers* to God! However, when Jesus died and the Temple's Holy of Holies curtain was torn in two from top to bottom by God (Mt. 27:51), God's presence with them in Jesus was confirmed. From that point on, interacting freely and joyfully with God was open to anyone who would turn their eyes upon Jesus and believe.

God's presence with us, His people, has reached even closer. When Jesus ascended into heaven and sat down at Father's right hand to rule (perhaps signified by the Ark in the true temple of God, Rev. 11:19), He did not leave us alone. He sent His Spirit to live *with* us—*in* us. **Believer's bodies** now house a person of the Trinity! "Do you not know that your bodies are temples of the Holy Spirit, who is in you, whom you have received from God? You are not your own; you were bought at a price. Therefore honor God with your bodies" (1 Cor. 6:19-20). Built around the cornerstone of Jesus, believers together are **His Church,** God's holy temple, "a dwelling in which God lives by his Spirit" (Eph. 2:19-21). God's law is written on our hearts (2 Cor. 3:2-3). We sing His praise and offer *prayers* to Him. Even if we are quarantined at home, comatose on a hospital bed, imprisoned in the darkest cell, or huddled in a refugee camp, God is *with* His children, His Spirit is *within* our bodily sanctuaries. The Bible assures us of this, sharing stories of God's answers to prayers in the direst of situations. Consider the experience of Hagar and Ishmael who were banished to the desert and found by God, "She gave this name to the Lord who spoke to her: 'You are the God who sees me.'" (Gen. 16:13). God heard and Ishmael became a great nation. Consider Jonah in the whale: "In my distress I called to the LORD, / and he answered me. / From deep in the realm of the dead I called for help, / and you listened to my cry" (Jonah 2:2). God heard and Jonah was vomited onto dry land and saved. Consider King Hezekiah who was dying and prayed, "Remember, O LORD, how I have walked before you faithfully and with wholehearted devotion and have done what is good in your eyes" (2 Kings 20:3). God heard and gave him 15 more years of life. Consider Paul and Silas who were in prison, "praying and singing hymns to God" (Acts 16:25). God heard and sent an earthquake that opened their jail cells; they went home to eat with their jailor and baptize him. May we be encouraged to always pray, confident that we can access God's care and His power through the Spirit. And even if we become unable to think or speak, God's Spirit within us can comfort our hearts and groan prayers on our behalf to Jesus and Father. We are never alone—God is with us!

WE are WITH OTHERS

In Genesis 2:18 we hear God say, "It is not good for the man to be alone." So God created Eve for Adam and together they created children who became the human race. Introvert or extrovert, we were all born into the care of others. Most of us have families that influence us. Additionally, we are part of a society that shapes our ways of living. We possess ways of communicating verbally or nonverbally. I have no doubt that God created us to interact *with others.*

God's Word is filled with teachings about how people are to live well with each other. Most important are the Old Testament's greatest commandments of which Jesus reminds us:

> "The most important one . . . is this: 'Hear, O Israel: The Lord our God, the Lord is one. Love the Lord your God with all your heart and with all your soul and with all your mind and with all your strength.' The second is this: 'Love your neighbor as yourself.'"

> (Mark 12: 29b-31)

The Bible also teaches believers that "there are many parts, but one body" (I Cor 12:12) and that we should have equal concern for each other. Praying *with* and *for* others is a way we love with God's love. Of the Bible's more than ninety "one another" verses, many call on us to pray. For example, the Apostle Paul writes: **"**Be devoted to one another in love. . . . Be joyful in hope, patient in affliction, **faithful in prayer** . . . . Bless those who persecute you; bless and do not curse. Rejoice with those who rejoice; mourn with those who mourn" (Rom. 12:10,12,14-15). He also writes: "Pray in the Spirit on all occasions with all kinds of prayers and requests. With this in mind, be alert and always keep on **praying for all the Lord's people**" (Eph. 6:18).

The Apostle James writes:

> Is anyone of you sick? Let them call the elders of the church to **pray** over them and anoint them with oil in the name of the Lord . . . . Therefore confess your sins to each other and **pray** for each other so that you may be healed. The **prayer** of a righteous person is powerful and effective.
>
> (James 5:14-16)

Like the men who tore up the roof to lower their friend in front of Jesus, we can zealously bring others before Jesus through prayer— even if they are miles away, even if they are unaware of our prayerful care, and especially if they are physically or mentally unable to pray. What a blessing to belong to a healthy community wherein we can name our needs, share our joys, lament over brokenness, and together seek God's powerful guidance!

Being *with* others in prayer happens all around us. Here are just a few examples from my experience:

> While waiting for my car to be serviced at the local dealership, I wandered past a counter holding a

basket filled with plastic toy soldiers. A sign on the basket read "PLEASE take a soldier home and place it somewhere that will remind you to PRAY for the Men and Women who have served and are currently serving our country."

***

In the 1980's, a couple from my church told me that they created weekly prayer lists. The lists included people and happenings that they deemed needy of prayer. Each day they would pray for the persons and causes listed for that day. Forty years later and in their nineties, that couple continues that practice. They are dedicated to a ministry of disciplined prayer-care.

***

When a friend's mother died, he came to my home and mourned, "I've lost my prayer warrior." He lived 300 miles away from his mom, but he knew that her prayers for God's wisdom in his work and for the Spirit's peace and joy in his life had sustained him.

***

My older brother was dying. He lay sedated in a hospital on the other side of the country. His daughters set up a speaker-phone conference-call. Placing the phone on his pillow, they asked me to sing to him his favorite prayer song, *How Great Thou Art*. I did, bringing us all together in prayer before God.

***

I write a "Prayer Matters" column for my church's weekly worship guide, providing prompts for congregants' prayers. Once a month I list the names of members who are in care homes. However, one month, I inadvertently left out a man's name. His distraught wife phoned me early Monday morning to advocate, "He still needs the church's prayers!" Of course he did; I included his name the next week.

***

In 1775, the Continental Congress set aside a day of prayer and in 1952, President Truman signed a bill proclaiming the National Day of Prayer into law. Now, on the first Thursday in May, people of all faiths are asked to pray for the concerns and work of our nation and its leaders.

***

Television news often reports on prayer vigils held during times of crisis, terrorism, horrific crime, natural disasters, mass murders, or sudden and senseless deaths. People gather around makeshift memorials of flowers, posters, and candles to pray, sometimes for total strangers.

***

My other brother was hospitalized with Covid-19 and its complications for more than 59 days. Scores of friends and family repeatedly posted on Facebook that they were praying. Our family felt so encouraged and blessed to be part of a community of prayer. God allowed him to recover and return home.

We are often alerted by the Holy Spirit to pray for someone even though we have not received a formal prayer request from them. I recall the day I recognized that the Holy Spirit does this. I had asked a friend to pray for a particular need and my colleague responded, "I will pray for you when the Spirit brings you to mind." At first I was nonplussed; I felt he was reluctant to pray and was seeking cover by blaming the Spirit. However, upon further reflection, I realized that his words accurately describe how prayer works. It is the Spirit Who initiates our mindfulness to pray for others. A person comes to mind or a need appears on social media or in the church bulletin or on the news, and our hearts feel "urged" to seek God's presence and power for a situation. That is the time to pray—on the spot, right then. Father is eager to shape both the subjects of the prayer and the doers of the praying. We don't want to miss out on the opportunity to grow in love and to strengthen our faith.

Besides the Spirit's urgings, reading God's Word to increase our understanding of Him and our understanding of His agenda helps shape our prayers. Even though His ways are past tracing out (Rom. 11:33), we may pray for His will. Praying trains our hearts to trust His power, His holiness, His past works of greatness, His love and forgiveness, and His timing. (Psalm 77 is a great example of this.)

While we need the Spirit's urgings and the Word's teachings to shape our prayers, it is also important to find motivation to pray in recognizing that God has given all of us the job of being praying people. Praying is a *Spirit-anointed role* to which God has called *every* believer, not just those who easily converse or who don't mind being up front. All believers' hearts are sanctuaries for the Spirit and all believers are called to become *priests* (I Pet. 2:5, cf. Rev. 5:10) within those sanctuaries. Priests sacrifice time and resources for the benefit of others. They act as prayer mediators between others and God. In doing so, we reflect Jesus.

The Bible describes Jesus as Prophet, Priest, and King. Among other actions, as *prophet*, Jesus spoke the Word into action (Mt. 13:57). As *king*, Jesus ascended to the Father's side and reigns over all (I Cor 15:20-28). As *priest*, Jesus sacrificed Himself as the perfect

Lamb for our sins. He grieves with us in our brokenness and sorrow. He teaches us to pray and continually prays for us to Father. He is One with Father's holiness in the temple of heaven (Heb. 4:14).

Because believers have been made holy by his death and represent the ascended Jesus on earth, we have been anointed with His Spirit's presence in our hearts to carry out these roles on His behalf until He comes again. We act as *prophets* when we speak the Word of God, share the Good News, and testify of God's power (1 Pet. 4:11). We carry out the *kingly* rule of God when we care for creation and work for God's peace and God's justice (Gen 2: 15, 19-20). We act as *priests* when we seek to honor the holiness of God in our bodies and when we sacrificially serve others, standing with them in their brokenness and despair and offering prayers on behalf of their souls and lives.

How good to know that Jesus experienced our human ways! He understands all the struggles within our bodies, minds, and souls. He knows both how precious and how difficult it is to deal with other people. He knows that life is an ongoing spiritual battle against the temptations and the destruction of the evil one. Not only does He know and understand, but He has the power to bring about change, relief, comfort, and restoration. As we come to Him and pray in His name for others, we are able to seek His wisdom and mercy in all situations and plead for His power and shalom to be evidenced in the lives of all. Coming alongside someone to pray in the Spirit brings them into God's presence when they may be too tired, too frightened, too confused, or too far from God to pray.

It is good to speak to God. Even when the situation is dire or a sin seems beyond salvation, our prayers evidence and encourage trust in God Who is restoring all things. When my mother was 13, her mother died of cancer and three months later, her father died of pneumonia. An orphan raised by siblings, she learned to deeply trust in God. Mom's favorite hymn was "What a Friend We Have in Jesus" written by Joseph Mendicott Scriven (1855). We had the second sentence engraved on her gravestone.

What a friend we have in Jesus,
all our sins and griefs to bear!
What a privilege to carry
everything to God in prayer!
O what peace we often forfeit,
O what needless pain we bear,
all because we do not carry
everything to God in prayer!
(https://hymnary.org/text/what_a_friend_we_have_in_jesus)

As priests for our time in history, we pray God's will and blessings for *friends, strangers, and enemies.* Almost every week I am alerted to a *friend's* serious struggle and am asked to pray. When I was a child, I am sure my parents prayed privately for serious concerns, but I don't recall us praying for other children or other families, even though there must have been children and families who struggled with racism, bullying, abuse, poverty, homelessness, perversion and corruption as there are now. Now, health concerns I never heard about as a child seem to touch every friend—cancer, disability, Alzheimer's, addictions, heart and weight problems, issues of sexuality and aging. And, unlike the days of my youth when television was new, media and technology now bombard me with awareness of influencers, issues, and opinions which my friends and I may hold differently. These things cause me to pray for wisdom, healing, protection, discernment, gentleness, and peaceful patience. The Apostle Paul would be happy to hear that; he speaks of putting away childhood talking, thinking, and reasoning so that we can love (and I would say—pray for) others:

Love is patient, love is kind. It does not envy, it does not boast, it is not proud. It does not dishonor others, it is not self-seeking, it is not easily angered, it keeps no record of wrongs. Love does not delight in evil but rejoices with the truth. It always protects, always trusts, always hopes, always perseveres.

(1 Cor. 13: 4-7)

Besides friends, we also can pray for *strangers*—the friend of a friend, needy people we see on the news or on the street, patients in passing ambulances or those waiting at some unknown destination for a blaring fire truck. We can prayer-walk our neighborhoods noting the toys, unkempt yards, or happy decorations and pray for the faith, safety, health, and joy of each home and all within. We can pray for those who attend surrounding schools and sister churches, asking God that they may learn and grow up well, using their skills and talents to bless the world. We can pray for agencies and their clients, seeking the efficacy of the aid they offer or receive— housing, food, jobs, training, and counseling. We can pray for those in authority locally, nationally, and worldwide. Even during hotly contested elections, we can pray for the integrity and welfare of all who are running and for the health of the nation. We can pray for the protection and steadfast witness of missionaries and the persecuted church. We can pray for the arts, that creative beauty and truthful meaning may be expressed and enjoyed. We can pray for the relief, release, refuge, provision, and protection of those dealing with disease, natural disasters, prison displacement, wars, trafficking, hunger, and ethnic cleansing. It does not matter that we don't know the names of these strangers; God does. He sees every person made in His image and He cares about them. He knows they need Jesus' rescue and the power of His indwelling Spirit. He created His Church to come alongside, to outpour His love through prayers and gifts of grace. The Apostle Timothy wrote: " I urge . . . that petitions, prayers, intercession and thanksgiving be made for all people—for kings and all those in authority, that we may live peaceful and quiet lives in all godliness and holiness" (I Tim. 2:1-2).

We also pray for our *enemies*—those towards whom we have ill feelings, those who have wronged and abused us, those who have killed what we love, those who hate God. This is not easy. Though our hearts ache, we seek to trust in God's sovereignty and pray that He will turn evil to good. Jesus said: "Love your enemies and pray for those who persecute you, that you may be children of your Father in heaven" (Mt. 5:44). Through the power of the Spirit, perhaps our hearts will find freedom from hatred as we plead for our enemies' health and welfare with Father. Through the power of the Spirit, maybe the enemy will be drawn to Jesus. In the power of the Spirit, maybe our prayers for enemies are preparing us to seek new opportunities to approach them, understand, and forgive. Or maybe, in the power of the Spirit, we will boldly cry out for God's justice against true evil as did King David and acknowledge that judgment and vengeance belong to the Lord. Whatever the case, we are called to pray, always seeking for God's will to be done. His will is for the best.

It can be a burden, but mostly it is a joy to be with others in prayer. Often our prayers for others will be private or one-on-one. However, when we offer prayers publicly—for others in the presence of others—we enlarge hope and widen testimony. As people read our prayers online, or hear us speak to God on their behalf, we are all drawn together into God's powerful presence. God's people can testify of His goodness and His mighty acts in their lives; in strength together we can carry forward His purposes and offer encouragement and help.

Just as I was writing these words, a spry 88-year-old friend walked up to my door to share the good news that her youngest son's DNA was a 100% match to her oldest son's DNA, providing hope that the oldest son's leukemia could be helped by a transfer of stem cells. "You have to give God all the credit! Whatever happens, God is in control," she said, smiling. "I think I'm still alive so that I can pray for them." Together we prayed a prayer of joyful thanks and hope for her family. Yes, praying braids us together into a strong cord of love and shalom (Ecc. 4:12).

From our youngest years to our last days, we may talk with the Trinity on behalf of others. To invite the Spirit's urgings and increase awareness of other's needs, consider these suggestions:

➢ Notice the needs of *children* and listen to the needs of their friends. Help children bring those needs to the Father—at the table, in the car, before bed. Help them pray for others.

➢ Encourage *aging saints* who are homebound or living in care homes to carry out the important work of praying for others, perhaps supplying them with a list of names or concerns.

➢ Make use of *prayer lists*, prayer requests, and worship guides to focus yourself on the needs of others.

➢ Each time you listen to *world news* or read the paper, rather than ruminating in confusion or fear, lift up the particular concerns to our God and King.

➢ Practice writing and praying *right-now prayers*. More on this in the next chapter!

WE are WITH GOD

In 1988, I was teaching at a Christian high school whose teams advanced to win the state championships in both girls' and boys' basketball. It was an exuberant, wonderful experience! We had spirit gatherings and wore blue and gold school colors; the fire department hosted a parade down Main Street; television and newspapers reported our "David and Goliath" story as our little school moved up through the ranks. Classes were cancelled so that everybody could drive three hours south to the arena. Hundreds of us screamed and chanted, stomped and clapped, waving printed signs of GO! FIGHT! WIN! Such a rush of breath and energy! And then—victory! We hugged and kissed friends and total strangers! What unity of purpose! What community! What success! What joy!

That's how I want to live with the Trinity and with other believers. The Merriam Webster online dictionary (https://merriam-webster. com) says that *enthusiasm* derives from a Greek word meaning "possession by a god." What a great word to describe believers— *enthusiastic*! Possessed by God! He created us, redeemed us, Spirit-filled us! As such, we can joyfully and powerfully pray together and *enthusiastically* cheer on God's good purposes: *GO! FIGHT! WIN!*

Think of all the worship songs that are prayers, many referencing Bible passages that adore and praise God. "Shout for joy to the Lord, all the earth" (Ps. 100:1). "Praise the LORD, O my soul; all my being, praise his holy name" (Ps. 103:1). "Let everything that has breath, praise the LORD. Praise the LORD" (Ps. 150:6). "Hallelujah! / Salvation and glory and power belong to our God . . . . Hallelujah! / For our Lord God Almighty reigns. / Let us rejoice and be glad and give him glory" (Rev. 19:1b, 6-7a)! We sing those words with gusto; why not add those lines to our prayers? Let's adore the Trinity, honor Their accomplishments, and call out Their majesty! Let's cheer God on and testify about His name!

One of my favorite vacation spots is Pismo Beach, California. I go there almost every year to walk the beach and talk with God. Years ago I began to practice a prayer ritual upon arriving at the water's edge: I stand with my toes in the water, lift my hands to the sky and sing the opening words of the Shane & Shane song "Lord, You're Beautiful" (© Universal Music-Brentwood Benson Publishing, Birdwing Music). This song and my stance before the rolling waves and expansive sky remind me that I am a beloved creature, living in the presence of my magnificent, loving Creator and heard by Him.

Besides adoring God, cheering prayers motivate us to *act* with the Trinity. Committed hearts don't just talk about love and faith; we seek to live them out (Eph 2:10). Jesus didn't just talk about Father; He claimed Father's authority and power. His words brought God's grace and love into action. When He said, "Be healed," the person was healed. When He called dead Lazarus to come out of the grave, Lazarus walked out alive. Jesus gave that power to the Twelve; how amazed they must have been when they first healed people or raised them from the dead (Acts 9:32-42)—especially after having earlier failed! Jesus assured them that if they had even mustard-seed-size faith, "nothing will be impossible for you" (Mt. 17:20).

I am still seeking to understand how such miraculous powers given to the disciples for signs and wonders are available to us. I believe those gifts were given to speed the spread of the gospel and I know they are evident in the ministries of others today, but I have not yet dared to pray so. However, I do pray confidently and boldly, and I try not to put all the work on God. I try to avoid always praying, "God, *You* bless them, comfort them, help them" because I want to remember that believers are called to take up our work as Kingdom agents for such a time as this (Es. 4:14). I try to pray: "Use *me* to comfort; use *us* to help." God is willing to work through us. Sometimes there is nothing that we can do except pray, but sometimes there is much we can do to help bring about the answers to our prayers. May we pray seeking God-empowered purposes.

Seeing God's great purposes in the Word and in the ongoing history of the church in the world is to focus on His-story (Eph 3: 10-12). When we see the big story of the Bible as *our* story in Christ, the motivation for prayer enlarges, the need for action enlarges, and the presence of hope enlarges. No person—believer or unbeliever—exists outside of God's story. How great is that? We are *with* God and He is *with* us and we are *with* each other making good choices that create and bless history! To visualize this with my students, I use my body, arms outstretched to create the timeline of history, my fingers pointing to eternity in both directions. My right arm represents B.C. times (Old Testament) and my left arm represents A.D. times (New Testament-present-future). My body cannot be extricated from this timeline! Standing tall, my head, torso, and legs, plus my outstretched arms, create a cross. That cross marks the coming of Jesus into history, changing the timeline from B.C. to A.D. It also marks the introduction of God's glorious Kingdom in Christ, which will fully be realized when He comes again. As a believer, I profess that my will has been crucified with Christ and I have been raised into Spirit-filled living with Him. Everything I do in my body will affect history—family life, friendships, schooling, jobs, leisure activities, community service and activism, worship, and more. My actions as a Kingdom prophet, king, and priest will bring consequences that are communal. How privileged and vital, then, to daily converse with the God of history about His plan and *my* part in it. How energizing and fulfilling to rejoice with God over powerful Kingdom victories! The Apostle Paul prays over the Ephesians and over us in this regard:

> I pray that out of his glorious riches he may strengthen you with power through his Spirit in your inner being, so that Christ may dwell in your hearts through faith. And I pray that you, being rooted and established in love, may have power, together with all the Lord's holy people, to grasp how wide and long and high and deep is the love of Christ, and to know this love that surpasses knowledge—that you may be filled to the measure of all the fullness of God.
>
> Now to him who is able to do immeasurably more than all we ask or imagine, according to his power that is at work within us, to him be glory in the church and in Christ Jesus throughout all generations, for ever and ever! Amen.
>
> (Eph 3:16-21)

Part Two

Talking with the Trinity
Publicly

RIGHT-NOW PRAYERS

Public prayers are prayed in the presence of others for others. Often we may be *assigned* to offer such a prayer, or *plan* to say such a prayer, or we may unexpectedly be *asked* to pray on-the-spot. In their shorter forms, such public prayers often take place at the start or ending of small group gatherings—meals, a committee meeting, a Bible study, or a compassion visit. If the person praying is in charge of the agenda, he or she has probably taken time to plan the prayer. Frequently, however, group members are requested to pray at a moment's notice. Because it feels awkward to refuse such a request, we often find ourselves scrambling for words, even while we are saying them! One of my friends combats the anxiety of such prayer requests by keeping a generic prayer in his Bible which he can read if he is suddenly volunteered. Another way to feel more prepared is to keep in mind a simple template, such as the one later in this chapter, which can help us shape the content of our prayers.

Public prayers also may happen when we feel the *urging of the Spirit* to pray *spontaneously* at the end of a conversation or in response to written correspondence. I suspect that when that urging comes, many of us have nervously opted out. We might be plagued by the discomfort of public speaking. We might imagine that the other person would feel judged or uncomfortable or would think us pious if we were to suggest prayer. We might cover our resistance to the Spirit's call with a vague promise, "I'll pray about that," or with a silent pledge that we will pray. However, if your experience is anything like mine, I often forget to pray once I've left the person or hung up the phone or turned off the computer.

I want to encourage us all to recognize our precious relationship with the Trinity, to become eager to hear Their call to pray with our neighbors, and to obey that call on the spot. I believe there is no more powerful way to love our neighbors than to walk with them into God's throne room and talk with Him. If we are talking on the phone or talking face-to-face and the other person shares a need, let's pray. If we receive emails or read Facebook posts in which our friends ask for prayers, let's respond by writing one. If we sense that the Spirit is calling us—right now—to bring needs before the LORD, let's do it!

If you have never prayed out loud for another person or never written a prayer for a person, now is a great time to prepare and practice. I was in my fifties and working for my church when I began to obey the Spirit's call to pray on the spot. Of course, not every conversation elicited prayer, but there were times when I was having deep conversations with others and I clearly sensed that they were aching for care. Swallowing my inexperience and discomfort, I began to ask, "How about if we pray about this right now?" Even over the phone I began to ask, "May I pray for you before I hang up?" Not once did anyone say "No." In fact, after the prayer, most people tearfully said "Thank you."

Right-now public prayers confirm to God that we need Him and want Him to be present in our present concerns. Father promises to listen to those who are washed clean in the blood of Jesus and are guided by the Holy Spirit. In His amazing grace, even non-believers whose hearts *seek* Him are heard. It fact, the Bible says the only prayers God is not fond of hearing are the prayers of those whose hearts are willfully against Him or who are performing (Mt. 6:5).

But I'm nervous to pray out loud!

Granted, we often think nervously about ourselves and about how others will perceive us, so it is helpful and wise to silently seek the Spirit's help in taking our focus off ourselves and placing it on the needs of others and on Jesus. We want our prayer to assure others that the Trinity is with us, right in that space, listening to us and loving us. And, of course, God already knows everything, so there is no need to put on airs with Him. No matter if we are desperate, doubting, babbling, crying, groaning, uncertain, questioning, or rejoicing—God will listen. Consider how easily you talk about your family members, your kids, your spouse, or your pets. That's the ease with which we may approach God to tell Him everything.

(Sometimes, I laugh and even respectfully joke with God, because I am convinced that He has a sense of humor.) We can run to *Abba* and be real—with the respect due His Name—talking to Him creature to Creator.

Although it may feel awkward at first, public praying becomes more comfortable with practice. If you are not used to hearing your voice out loud, consider practicing by praying your personal prayers out loud in the privacy of your room. Most evenings after I turn off the television, I stay in my chair and talk my evening prayer out loud to God. Another option is to practice constructing prayers as did the precious small group of women in the Bible study I lead. Although they all prayed privately, when we first started, not everybody was comfortable praying out loud. As we studied His Word, we came to know that God is alive, that He loves us, and that He has the power to guide and help us. We wanted to talk to Him together, so we shyly began to practice by taking turns speaking out loud around the table: "Let's pray **one sentence praising God** for something we see about Him in the Word or in our lives." (*I praise you, God, for being such a magnificent Creator!*) "Let's pray **one sentence thanking God.**" (*Thank you, God, for helping me find a doctor to diagnose my headaches.*) "Let's pray **one sentence asking God** for something that we trust He would like to give us." *(Lord, please calm my dad as he moves into a care home.)* Soon we expanded to "**a compliment and a request**" and so on. When we realized that talking out loud to God sounded just like talking to one of the Bible study women around the table, praying became easier.

What do I say when I pray for others?

Prayers for others arise out of good *listening.* Whether talking over the phone, face-to-face, or on social media, we carefully and respectfully listen to others as they express their joys, worries, hopes, and fears. We notice non-verbal messages such as their pauses, their sighs, and their tears. Hopefully, we take all this in without giving unasked for advice or expressing judgment (although inwardly we may be discerning and weighing the facts and asking the Spirit for wisdom). Hopefully, we've kept the focus on them, resisting our desires to steal the conversational ball or "top" their story. Then, when the time is right, the Holy Spirit will signal us; our loving hearts will yearn to carry the other's concerns to God. We will recognize that we both need to converse with Father Who created us, Jesus Who saved us, and the Spirit Who guides us. We are ready to pray.

First, we will want to ask permission from our friend to pray for him or her out loud ("Do you mind if I pray about this right now?"). Next, we will silently ask the Holy Spirit to give us words (*Holy Spirit, help me, please*). David did so: "May my prayer be set before you like incense; / may the lifting up of my hands be like the evening sacrifice. / Set a guard over my mouth, LORD; / keep watch over the door of my lips" (Ps. 141:2-3). The Spirit is willing to process our words into sweet-smelling "incense," but whatever words we use, they don't need to be fancy or pious. Our prayer will be shaped by what we have heard.

In addition, I keep in mind the template below. A *template* is a guide or pattern when one making something. An easy pattern for right-now prayers might include some or all of these elements, in any order:

- ✓ **Thanks** (for God's love and other good things)
- ✓ **Specific needs**/requests
- ✓ **Support for others** (spouses, doctors, caretakers)
- ✓ Trust for God's **will** and His **timing**
- ✓ Desire for God's **glory** to shine
- ✓ **"in Jesus name"**

POSTING WRITTEN PRAYERS

When friends ask for prayers in an email or on social media, I usually choose to write and send an *actual prayer*. I avoid saying "I'll pray for you" or posting a string of emojis. Why? I think there are several benefits to seeing a prayer in writing. When people ask for prayers, they are often stressed and feeling alone, unable to quiet their minds or trust the focus of their own prayers. Reading a prayer helps them *rest in the quiet assurance of another's words.* Also, the receiver can read the prayer *again and again*, each time coming before Father. Further, if the written prayer is posted online, it can become a *testimony* to the larger audience about God's power and love. Finally, because a posted prayer reaches a wide audience, it invites everyone into a *communal* conversation with God (evidenced by elicited "Amen!" replies). For all these reasons, I strongly encourage believers to write and post public prayers online.

If you have never done this, let me share a few examples of public prayers I have written. I think you will see how the template above plays out. I have substituted dashes for names.

I posted this prayer on social media in response to my brother's move from Covid hospitalization to rehab:

Lord Jesus,

We praise and thank you for this restoration. Please continue to strengthen ___, giving him strong lung capacity, sturdy muscles, and protection from germs. May he return home soon and thrive there, too. We trust Your will in his life.

In Your name,

Amen

This prayer was posted on social media in response to a mom's concerns about her child's **neurological health and tests:**

LORD Jesus,

You know exactly what is happening inside _____. Please help the doctors see it, understand it, and effectively treat it.

Please replace fear with trust in Your power.

In Your name I pray,

Amen.

I included this prayer in a **birthday** card mailed to a friend:

Talking with the Trinity

Dear Lord,

Thank you for the life of ____. He may be 80, but he is very much your child. You have his name written on the palm of your hand. You know when a hair falls from his head.

Bless ____ with Your protection and Your provision. May he rest secure in Your love. Please give him many more years of life and health. Please give him laughter and continued joy. May ____ always know that he is loved.

In Jesus' Name,
Amen.

As **wildfires** erupted around California in August 2020, I felt the Spirit's call to post this prayer on social media:

LORD God,

May it be Your will to contain the fires all around. Please protect and refresh the firefighters, working so faithfully in this record-breaking, oppressive heat.

Also, so many people are without homes due to fires, storm destruction, job loss, addictions, and so on. May Your abundance bless all agencies of care who are feeding and housing. Open all our hearts to compassion and generosity and aid.

In Jesus' Name.
Amen.

When the Covid-19 pandemic led to **facility quarantine** at Bethany Home for the aging, I emailed this longer prayer to the administrator and fellow members of the Board:

LORD Jesus,

Thank You for Bethany Home. Thank You for moving hearts to care for others, to create this place, to bring support to this ministry. Thank You for the administration. Please heal those from the office who are ill. Please give safety to ____ and staff and chaplains as they must continue their work and their interactions. Fill them with Your Spirit so they might overflow with hope and peace and love.

Thank you for the firm controls and precautions being taken to protect all staff and residents. Please place a hedge of protection around the places of Bethany's ministry, that no one will fall ill with this virus if it is Your will.

Please give strength to the caretakers who so faithfully come to work. May their times away from work give them rest and joy. As they go home and come back to work, please help them be cautious and clean. May their interactions with residents provide encouraging times to share faith and laughter.

Please bless all the residents and keep them healthy. This is not the first time any of them have felt confined, for age does that to us all, but this confinement brings to them little from the outside world, so life seems much smaller. Please open their memories to joys of the past. Thank you for their trust and love for their caretakers. May they find rest in their trust in You.

Please ease concerns for residents that many outside of Bethany's walls may have. May they trust that wise decisions are being made. May they seek to connect through mail, window visits, and phone calls so that the residents may know they are never alone or forgotten.

Risen Lord, You created us to live here, but you also promise us life eternal. We hold dearly to the present and to the promise. We trust in Your care. We seek Your protection.

Have mercy on Your world, Father, and give us joy even in these new ways of living. We wait for your healing and the freedom to live life fully, both here and with You.

In Your powerful Name,
Amen.

CREATING LONG PRAYERS

Public prayers are often part of *formal occasions* such as dedications, anniversaries, and worship services. They happen in front of a group in which most recognize that there is a God Who creates, controls, and sustains life; a God Who should be acknowledged and thanked for what is taking place.

Though many of us shake our heads and nervously back away from public speaking, I encourage you to write out longer conversations with the Trinity and simply *read* them. Such writings help a larger audience talk to God as one and serve as *crafted* offerings to the LORD. Perhaps creating a prayer to be "read with expression" seems to suggest a prideful performance; after all, didn't Jesus warn against the publican praying on the street corners (Mt. 6:5)? I believe Jesus was warning about the publican's heart—his public pride and lack of repentance—not his action of praying, but I do resonate with the fear of turning praying into performance. Given a platform, a crowd, and a microphone, many of us might be tempted to forget that God is our audience. So, how shall we remain focused and humble in the important task of mediating a conversation between God and a crowd? How shall we shape our love of words and the Word into priestly petitions rather than performances to gain praise?

I believe that God accepts our prayers however they are crafted. I might liken them to creating homemade Valentines; we try to avoid glue smears and crooked writing, but we know that the receiver will delight in them regardless. Just so, I hope that we will want to try to give God our best expressions of love, artisanship, honor, and partnership. As we ponder life and faith, we will become more proficient at crafting a lovely longer prayer. This chapter suggests ways to shape the *content* of a longer public prayer.

First, seek the Trinity through the Holy Spirit.

We prepare for prayer by asking the Spirit to tune our heart to the Father and to the Son. We ask the Spirit to lead us to the right words. Many ideas that come to our minds have merit, but we also know that our biased opinions can get in the way. We don't want to pray something that misunderstands God's ways and will.

As we write, we listen for the Spirit's urgings. The gentle whisper of God that Elijah heard can be recognized (I Kings 19:12). We need to be ready to edit as He leads. (I have removed whole paragraphs from my prayers and from this book because I sensed the Spirit was sighing about my babble.) Such leading is humbling, but also refreshing. We can trust Him.

Greet our Great God.

The Audience of our prayer, the Receiver, is always God. We are praying to the Triune God Whom we honor and adore. We may address Him by any of His many names. We invite His attention. We greet Him as we would any dear one to whom we open our door.

The fact that "adoration" begins the well-known acronym A.C.T.S. (Adoration, Confession, Thanksgiving, Supplication) reminds us that much can be said to God *before* we ask Him to supply our needs. We can lavish the Trinity with love, affirmation, and adoration. Feel free to use the list below, or find other truths found in the Word, for ideas and words with which to to compliment our Three-in-One God. (To remind you of the ever-present Trinity within the Godhead, I am deliberately mixing references to God and Trinity):

> God is the only God.
> God is One in Trinity, three Persons of one essence.
> The Trinity exists beyond time, Alpha and Omega,
> from eternity to eternity.
> The Trinity Persons have many names, among them:
> Shield, Tower, Savior, King of Kings, Holy God,
> Comforter, Deliverer, Almighty, Rock, Jealous,
> Immanuel, Cornerstone, Redeemer, Prince of Peace,
> Messiah, Lamb, Word, Bright and Morning Star.
> The Trinity is everywhere present.

God controls and allows all happenings.

The Trinity has accomplished great acts throughout history.

The Trinity created the universe, all things and systems in it. Nature answers to God.

God commands angel hosts, wins battles, rides with the cherubim on the chariots of the wind.

God speaks through His Word reminding us of His great acts, of His will and His holiness, of our sin and His salvation.

God knows everything; there's no need to hide our thoughts, actions, or feelings.

God is only good; His will is for all that is uplifting and positive such as joy, hope, peace, and love.

God creates endless variety, minute detailing, awesome beauty, glorious splendor.

The Trinity loves us and enters into unchanging, faithful covenant relationship with us.

The Trinity gifts us with talents and abilities to use for God's glory and the good of others.

God gives abundance, beyond all that we could ask or think.

God has won the victory over the evil one; He will judge and destroy all evil.

God is with us, bringing His Word to mind, empowering us to do His will as agents of His Kingdom.

The Trinity is coming again with glory to make all things made new.

The Trinity will live forever with believers.

Echo God's Word.

The source for seeking God's will and ways is the Spirit-breathed Word. It is wise to ask the Spirit to point you to the parts of the Word that He wants you to reflect on or quote; He is willing to bring such passages to mind. Reciting the Word to God confirms that we hear Him, believe Him, trust Him, and honor Him.

God's Word records the *truths that shape us*—our identity, our history, our confessions of sin, our joy in forgiveness, our requests for provision, our paths to love and justice. God's Word is also full of *imagery* that we can reference in our prayers. The great and unfathomable God reveals Himself, graciously likening Himself to understandable things such as the tower, the rock, the seed, the wind, the fire, the hen with her chickens. Jesus also used everyday items and situations to illustrate His parables and describe His I AM name. Years ago I attended a prayer seminar led by free-lance writer, Edith Bajema. In her handout entitled "Imagery in the Language of Worship" (used with permission) she wrote:

> First, choose one image that tells something about God. . . . Set the timer for five minutes and write down every word or phrase that comes to mind in connection with that image . . . . Don't edit or debate it at this point. When you've got your list, choose several words or phrases that are especially meaningful to you or that seem to carry the most power. Think about how they relate to God's character and how that relates to your needs as a congregation or to the way you want to praise God. Then write a brief prayer (40 words or less), using the image and word picture . . . . Let people sense the power of that image and the mystery of how God connects with it in their lives.

Consider the occasion.

• Are you crafting a *weekly* prayer for church worship? Sunday-to-Sunday prayers often mention the needs and concerns of members; the church's outreach, education, and fellowship activities; the present experience of worship such as music, preaching, and the offering. The week's world news will need the church's prayers, too.

• Are you celebrating a *day on the liturgical calendar or the sacraments*? You may wish to reference the Gospel's good news celebrated on Christmas, Good Friday, Easter, Pentecost, Ascension Day, the Lord's Supper, or baptism. Prayers can be shaped around visuals connected with those events such as the angels, the cross, the empty tomb, the fire and wind, the eyes unto heaven, the bread and wine, the water of life.

• Are you praying on the occasion of the *culture's special days* such as Thanksgiving, Mothers' Day and Fathers' Day, Independence Day, Labor Day, Election Day, or the beginning and end of the school year? Prayers can give thanks for these celebrations as God's good gifts and also recognize that God desires certain actions and attitudes related to these experiences.

• Are you celebrating a *special event*—rejoicing in a new pastor; celebrating an anniversary, wedding, graduation, new job; ordaining a new pastor; welcoming new members or church board members; commissioning a mission team; or welcoming a missionary? Prayers may celebrate God's faithfulness, mention specific people from the past or present, call for the Spirit's empowerment, and look forward to the future.

• Are you gathering for *lament or death?* The Psalms exemplify ways to ask God difficult questions and express anguish. Despite His victory over the evil one, God allows the consequences of evil to be present in our world for a time. We long for God's restoration of all things. We struggle to know how to bring help, justice, hope, life and light as His agents. Yet, until He comes again, we trust in His promises and His power and our prayers will seek His rule, His guidance, and His miracles.

Consider who is meeting with God.

Public prayers seek to join people with God. It is good to remember that while believers claim the same LORD and read the same Word, each has his or her own personality, experiences, perspectives, politics, and faith expressions. Consider how differently these persons might hear your words and choose appropriately:

- a believer *versus* an unbeliever
- a child *versus* an aging saint
- a believer overtaken by sin *versus* a believer who confesses daily
- a person grieving or lonely *versus* people surrounded by family and friends
- a person facing job loss or having little money *versus* a person getting a raise
- someone exhausted or angry *versus* someone active in exciting options
- someone addicted or trying to break a habit *versus* those who are fit and clean
- those married *versus* those single or widowed
- those devastated by disaster or fearful of the future *versus* those snug and secure
- believers active in social justice *versus* those who are passive
- people of different political views

When we bring others before God, we are humbly seeking His truth together. To avoid speaking with insensitivity or judgment, it is good to ask the Spirit to tune our hearts to love and compassion. For what are others yearning to receive from God? What are they feeling? What words do we need to temper? How can we pray with compassion and without being patronizing? In another handout delightfully titled "Guidelines for Putting Words in the Congregation's Mouths" (used with permission), Edith Bajema warns:

Not everyone feels the way you do toward God. Not everyone has the same sins to confess, the same sense of failure or commitment or faith or doubt . . . . A prayer is not a sermon, an argument for a certain position, or an explanation or commentary . . . . When we write prayers— especially prayers of confession—we should assume the best of the congregation, not the worst . . . . [Rather than cover] the congregation with a blanket condemnation of guilt and irresponsibility . . . simply confess that the desire to sin is strong in us— and that we give in to it at times.

I want to encourage us again to pray for *specifics* that fit the audience. It is common to name a subject, give thanks for it, and request a generic blessing on it such as: "Thank You for our missionaries; please bless them. We pray for those in war-torn countries; please bless them." God *does* already knows what is needed and it *is* a blessing to name something before the LORD and to give thanks, but I am struck by Jesus' penetrating interaction with two blind men pleading for mercy. Jesus' question was: "What do you want me to do for you?" They responded with the specifics: "We want our sight" (Mt. 20: 32-33), and that sight was the specific miracle that Jesus provided. I believe it is helpful to spend time considering the specific things needed and name them before the LORD. If it is in His will, He promises, "If you have faith and do not doubt . . . if you believe, you will receive whatever you ask for in prayer" (Mt. 21:21-22). This is the wonder and intimacy of our God Who cares about each of us so much that He counts "the very hairs of your head" (Luke 12:7).

Finally, consider the time frame.

As with most things in life, less is better. Precision, concision, and propriety are always good guidelines. Those of us who love words will need to keep pruning, asking the Spirit for guidance so that rather than blab or blunder, we bless.

DELIVERY

As a former teacher of public speaking, I feel compelled to add a few suggestions about preparing and reading prayers:

- To more easily see your prayers, print them in a 14-point bold font. Underline, embolden, or capitalize key words for emphasis. Consider where slight pauses will help ideas sink in, and mark or space those spots.
- Practice reading your prayer out loud at home to hear how it flows and where it trips you up. Make minor adjustments. Ask the Holy Spirit to lead you.
- Once you are up in front, look the people in the eyes, smile, and invite them to join you in prayer ("Would you please pray with me?" "Let's pray to our God.")
- Reading too quickly will not allow your words time to sink in. Reading words without expression will not touch the hearts and minds of the audience. Calm yourself and find a comfortable, thoughtful pace that will help others see the pictures you have created and think along with your words. Express sincere emotions. Emphasize precious words. (Consider the voices and energy with which you read *Goldilocks and the Three Bears* to children; read your prayer with that level of engagement.)
- When the service is over and people thank you for your prayer, accept it and enjoy the moment with the Spirit!

May your prayers hug the audience and the Persons of Trinity, breathe with Their life, see with Their eyes, love with Their heart, and pulsate with Their power.

TEMPLATES
FOR LONGER PUBLIC PRAYERS

For an entire year, I experimented with praying worship prayers without using notes. I would meditate on pertinent subject areas before time, then pray off-the-cuff about items from a simple outline in my head. However, after forgetting needs and names, and on one occasion trying to pray against unfaithful behavior, but being hard-pressed to remember Isaiah's word "dung" and instead choosing the shocking synonym "cow pies" (for which I later apologized in the church newsletter), I returned to scripting my prayers.

Using a template helps me shape my prayers. A template guides my mind and the minds of the audience into paths of logic and rhythmic flow. Certain templates explore God's images and metaphors; they invite our mind's eye to see in new ways and call our hearts to feel deeply. Certain templates resemble cheers, showcasing aspects of God's glorious complexity, raising our spirits to praise and adore Him. Certain templates point out wrongs and call for help or renewed commitment.

It is true that God nowhere commands outlined prayers. I suppose we could simply come into *Abba's* arms babbling; He welcomes loving, trusting hearts seeking Him even when we are confused. However, God also created this world with infinite beauty, variety, and order. I believe that well-constructed prayers of faith, hope, and joy delight Him, too.

Templates can be shaped as lists, categories, sequences, parallel structures, refrains, reversals, repetitions, and word-play. If you've read this far, you know that I believe that when we ask the Spirit to guide us, we can expect His urging—in this case, toward a template. The following suggestions only scratch the surface, but they may be helpful to you as you seek a way to structure your prayer and guide the attention of the audience:

- Chronology: eternity, past, present, future, eternity.
- The Lord's Prayer

- Adoration, Confession, Thanksgiving, Supplication (A.C.T.S.)
- Biblical visual images/metaphors such as "tower," "fire," "rock," "trees"
- Biblical injunctions: see, know, believe, turn, trust, go, speak
- Biblical history: creation, fall, redemption, renewal, glorification
- Church ministries: worship, education, outreach, service, fellowship, prayer
- Ages: infant, childhood, youth, college and career, parental, middle age, retirement, old age
- Life arenas: government (local and national); economics; first responders (military, police, fire); agencies of care (adoptive, counseling, hospitals); schools; jobs; homes; churches/ missionaries; leisure
- Senses: hearing, sight, taste, smell, touch
- Body: physical, emotional, spiritual
- God's "body": eyes, ears, nostrils, mouth, wings, arms, hands, feet
- Word juxtaposition such as Creator/creature, life/death, formation/reformation/transformation, heaven/earth
- "We receive from You"/ "We release to You" (palms up/palms down prayer)
- Old Testament, New Testament, Church today
- Themes/quotations from hymns/choruses or Scripture
- The Trinity and their areas of work: Father (Creation, Providence), Son (Salvation, Kingship), and Holy Spirit (Calling, Teaching).
- Characteristics of God: all-knowing, all-powerful, everywhere present, only good
- Truths about God: living, reigning, covenanting, victorious
- Names of God: Almighty, Lamb, Prince of Peace, Word, Alpha/ Omega

A Compilation of
LONGER PRAYERS

The following prayers are arranged to roughly follow the chronology of a calendar year. They were written and offered—most during worship services—by members of my church (used with permission) and by me (all undesignated prayers are mine). You will notice that each author has his or her own writing style and faith vocabulary. You will hear our various "voices" in our prayers.

I am including these prayers for several reasons. First, friends suggested that I compile many of my prayers. Secondly, these prayers demonstrate how a theme can be developed and how a template can structure a prayer. Most importantly, I believe that reading these prayers will draw you into devotional time with God. In that regard, I believe your experience with these prayers will be richer if you sample them one at a time, over time, rather than scanning them all in one sitting. While they may contain similar phrases and vocabulary, each was created for a unique worship service, weeks or years apart from the others, so some space is needed to allow each to breathe with power in its own right.

I have removed most of the time-bound concerns that these prayers contained because they reflected my particular church family, yet I indicated where those concerns were included, so that if you use these prayers, you might choose to insert your own church family needs in those places. I retained references to ministries that I thought were common to most churches.

If you are responsible to pray worship prayers, please feel free to edit these prayers for use in your worship services. Most take 7-10 minutes to read aloud. (Their length led me to print them in smaller font here.) Feel free to lift phrases or templates to become part of your prayers.

I believe these prayers were inspired by the Spirit and belong to Him. As you read them, may you delight in talking with the Trinity!

FACING THE NEW YEAR

Father in Heaven,

I want to live this New Year with Your vision.
I realize that I my "old man" self must continue to die.
I want to be the "new man" in Christ.
Strengthen my resolve to keep my body healthy,
so it will have energy to serve with you.
Keep my mind pliable, open and instructed,
so I will have Your compassion.
Breathe on me until I hear your voice
and understand your Word, following Your will.
Open my eyes to the needs of my brothers and sisters
in this church and in this world.
Fill me with the mighty rushing of Your Spirit,
so I cannot help but act and stretch myself to love as You.
Do what You must to keep me close;
You know how I wander, dawdle, and try to run in front of You.
Rid me of encumbrances of the past –
disappointments, losses, fears, failures.
Remind me that You have conquered Satan, sin, and death;
their power is void; their pain is fleeting.
Teach me to trust with hope, for in You there is
always and forever grace, restoration, joy, and power.
It's a new year! I want to go for it with you, Lord!
Let's knit this Body ever more tightly into a garment
of care, warmth, forgiveness, and encouragement!
Let's fill this sanctuary
with powerful preaching and exuberant praise!
Let's make this church unstoppable
in loving and serving our town and the world!
Let's do things only You can dream of!
Let's go for it, Lord. I'll follow Your lead.

Amen.

NEW CALENDAR YEAR

Mighty God,

You are beyond time, but You know what the future holds,
because You hold it in Your kingly hand.
On this New Year's Day, we praise You as the only God,
the true and living God,
the Creator of all that is.
We praise You that regardless of our schedules and timelines,
all our times are in Your hands.
We praise You for proving that life in the future can be
refreshed, resurrected, and restored.
Thank you for that HOPE!
Thank You for being our good and loving Father,
watching over us and providing all we need.
Thank You for the gift of salvation in Jesus.
Thank You for the Spirit living within us to teach and guide us.
Thank you for your Word, Your power, Your love and mercy.

Thank You, too, for the gifts of home families and church families
with whom we may connect and celebrate.
It is good to make memories, recount stories, give and receive love.
It is good to have the care and prayers of others
as we journey through life.

This morning we ask for a special measure
of Your peace, wisdom, and healing presence for . . .
(List member needs.)

Dear Jesus, please refresh us in 20___.
Cleanse our hearts anew and guide us in restoring order to our lives.
Motivate us to sweep out unhealthy and unloving habits.
Expose the filth and waste we have accumulated
and lead us to purity.
Remind us of how we have been forgiven,
and empower us to forgive others.
Tutor us to grow in Your ways of compassion and justice.
As we submit to You, please cast out evil and occupy us.
Take up residency in each heart, so there is no room for the Accuser.

Then, please tune our hearts to sing Your praise.
May we live with joyful courage because we walk with You.

LORD Jesus, please give this church clarity about how we should
proceed—in preaching and administration, in education and outreach,
in youth programs and worship, in care and fellowship.
Ready us to shine as a light in this community.

Holy God, despite natural disasters, governmental upheaval,
losses of life and dignity, economic uncertainty,
and many other fears and sins within our nation and our world,
we trust that Your will continues to unfold.
Please bring success to all efforts forged in goodness.

Lord Jesus, please shape us and use us to be eager agents of change,
agents of prayer, agents testifying of Jesus' presence in our lives.
Please impart to us brightness, energy, laughter and singing,
so that all who see and hear us—even in the small things
or the hard times—may see Your glory and realize that in this dark
world there exists a church of hope and joy, hugging and helping.

> *Another year is dawning! / Dear Father, let it be,*
> *in working or in waiting, / another year with thee . . . .*
> *Another year of progress / another year of praise,*
> *another year of proving / Thy presence all the days . . . .*
> *Another year is dawning! / Dear Father, let it be,*
> *on earth, or else in heaven, / another year for thee.*
> [Francis R. Havergal, 1874,
> (https://hymnary.org/text/another_year_is_dawning)

We love you, LORD.
Thank you for hearing our prayer in the strong Name of Jesus,
Amen.

TEMPLATE: RELEASE AND RECEIVE

Invite the audience to employ two symbolic actions: first, PALMS DOWN, **releasing** to God all that overwhelms; then, PALMS UP, eager to **receive** all that the LORD gives.

Triune, Supreme, Almighty God:

You create all things and sustain them.
As spiritual warfare continue, and evil fills this world,
we are confident in Jesus, our Savior and Conqueror.
You alone, O God, are King and Judge—forever.
Your perfect will is our good law.
Thank You that You are also our loving ABBA,
calling and equipping us to be agents of your Kingdom.
Thank you for traveling ahead of us and providing angels.
Thank you for revealing Truth in the Bible.
Thank you for placing Your Spirit in our hearts
to carry our prayers and teach us how to live your agenda.

*PALMS DOWN, we **release** to you*
all that hinders us from shining with Your glory:
our exhausting attempts to control
what You have not called us to manage;
our hopelessness about how to change a culture
idolizing possessions and sex;
our worries—about income, health, housing,
schooling, relationships, and safety;
our helplessness in the face of floods, fires, and drought;
our angst over world politics, rulers, and economies;
our fears of people who are different from us.
We release to you
our despair that people are suffering and dying due to
natural disasters, terrorism, racism, war, refugee life, crime, substance
abuse, and their dedication to military duty and law enforcement.
We release to you the care and protection of
(list individuals with specific needs)
and of all members, programs, and missionaries of this church family.

And now, for a few moments of SILENCE,
   we release to You our INDIVIDUAL concerns: _____
   (Pause for silent prayers — 20 seconds)

Lord, You are King. You are in control. You are love.

*PALMS UP, we open our hands to **receive** from your abundance:*
   Create in us clean hearts; renew a right spirit within us.
   Teach us the lessons of trust, patience, creativity, joy, and hope.
   We claim Your promises such as You knowing when a hair falls from
   our heads and You preparing a place for us after death.
   We receive with joy this place to gather for worship,
   teaching, fellowship, service, and outreach.
   We receive this blessed body of believers—people with whom to
   worship and pray, laugh and serve.
   Holy Spirit, may we receive Your guidance
   as we open the Word and pray.
   Jesus, we accept Your invitation to the Table this morning
   to receive the benefits of Your death on the cross

And now, for a few moments of SILENCE,
   we seek to receive INDIVIDUAL blessings: _____
   (Pause for silent prayers—20 seconds)

We love you, LORD.
   Thank you for hearing our prayers
   in the Name of the Father, Son, and Holy Spirit.

Amen.

BRIEF CHURCH WORSHIP PRAYER

Lord God,

Thank you for calling us here today,
not to hear from an ancient book,
but to be cut by Your living Word;
not to attend a memorial service for a dead teacher,
but to be challenged by our living LORD;
not to view our children's mobile of Pentecost doves,
but to respond to Your Living Breath.
It is true that we sit here, very different from each other,
some eager, some exhausted, some distracted.
We have private concerns regarding health, family,
relationships, loneliness, work, and finances.
But we thank You that You know our needs and will help us.
You have brought us here to experience the joys of community,
with You and with each other.
Your Word reminds us of Your character and Your will.
We will feel again Your embrace of grace.
As a body of believers, we will learn from each other today,
and care and pray for each other.
Thank you for calling us to serve our community.
We are striving to do that through
our USDA Food Giveaway,
our TSA Shelter meals,
the Redwood Home for moms and kids,
and the Sierra Salem homes for those with special needs.
Please continue to give us vision
and abundant resources for these ministries.
Thank you for your world, for its beauties and its challenges.
In these days of hurricanes and political unrest,
awaken our obedient spirits to pray, speak out, support, and go.

In the Name of Jesus,

Amen.

BRIEF CHURCH WORSHIP PRAYER

Dear LORD,

thank You for being here and everywhere—
alive, risen, ruling. Thank You for being only good and true.
Thank you for waking us to this new day and for the privilege of being
together here today. Thank you for the light and truth of Your Word.
May Pastor's Lenten messages change us.

Since we gathered last week, many things have happened.
You know them all. Many of us have talked with you about them all
week, but we bring them before you again this morning, because You
have given us this respite at the foot of the cross to lay our burdens down
and find rest in You. (List of items)

Please wash us,
heal us,
feed us,
calm us,
refresh us,
teach us.
Take away our fears and give us the laughter of grace.

Thank you for placing us within the fellowship and prayers of these
brothers and sisters in Christ. Use us to touch the lives of others
so that this week they may see and know that they are
not alone, but supported;
not hated or disliked, but loved and forgiven;
not desperate, but hopeful;
not owned by death, but moving toward eternal life.

Spirit of the living God, move us to reflect Jesus.
Rule us as Prince of Peace, Lord Jesus.
Take all the glory.
With Your angels, we adore and praise you.

Amen.

HUMAN COMPLEXITY
The beginning of a prayer by **John Nydam**

O Lord,
we come to you in prayer because You are our God.
There is none like You and, in fact, there is no other God.
You have searched us and You know us.
You are aware of all our comings and goings.
You know all of our thoughts, and even before we speak,
You know exactly what we are going to say.
You know how we feel—physically, emotionally, and spiritually.
Such intimate knowledge is too lofty for us
to attain or even understand.
Your Presence is always with us.
There is nowhere we can go that You are not there with us.
We can travel the globe like never before in history.
We can explore the deep depths of the ocean
in sophisticated diving pods which are able to sustain
extreme pressures—and You are there.
We can climb the mountain heights, even go to the top
of Mount Everest—and You are there.
We can even go to the moon and beyond and not even come close
to reaching the outer limits of Your Presence.
As we go through each day, aware of You
and looking for Your presence with us,
we become thankful and full of praise
for how You reveal Yourself to us in so many different ways.

Physically, You have given us bodies and minds
that can do so many different things—
from working with computers, to farming,
to working in the medical field, to educating in the classroom,
to working in businesses and stores and restaurants.
Even in our leisure time
there is such a vast array of activities we can enjoy.
When our bodies break down,
You have even given us the ability to heal.
Thank You for all these physical abilities You have given us.

Emotionally, Your Presence is always near as well.
Your guiding hand is there
when we are confused, not knowing which way to turn.
When we are fearful,
Your great power provides the confidence we need.
When we are having an exciting fun-filled day,
You are there to share it and receive our praise.
When we go through times of sorrow or despair,
Your comforting Spirit strengthens and revives our souls.
You are the Great Physician,
Who always knows what we need and when.

Spiritually, You guide us:
You have given us the Bible which we can read, study,
and turn to in order to find direction, meaning,
and encouragement for our daily lives.
Most importantly, we can find in it
Your story of salvation and forgiveness made possible
through the work of Your Son, Jesus Christ.
You have also given us Your Spirit to live within us.
What an incomprehensible gift—-that You,
the Lord of all things in heaven and on earth—
would make Your dwelling within us!
Lord, we are overwhelmed!
Transform us through Your Spirit
and make us more and more to be like Christ.
Direct and fill our lives, and give us of Yourself
so that we may bring praise and glory to Your name.

In Jesus Name,

Amen.

TEMPLATE: KINGDOM AGENTS—THIS WEEK

Father, Son, and Holy Spirit,

Thank you for calling us to this worship service
and encouraging us to interact with You.
Thank you for revealing Your will and ways in the Bible,
in the world, and in our hearts.
You are the One true and good God—
alive and on the move;
in control of all things;
victorious over sin, Satan, and death—
a God of forgiving love.
Thank you that your Kingdom is already here,
although we see it only in part.

Father, *Please heal our world. USE US AS AGENTS to proclaim and help establish your kingdom.*

• *Please make us cognizant of the ways we waste and abuse the abundant resources of Your earth.*

   This week, show each of us one new way we could
   conserve or protect our environment.
   We want to be STEWARDING agents of your kingdom.

• *Please open us to increased compassion in dealing with others here and around the world. Thank you for compassionate people —doctors and nurses, counselors and caretakers, and friends who bless us with care.*

   This week, place each of us in situations where we may dignify,
   help, and come alongside others.
   We want to be LOVING agents of your kingdom.

• *Please speak truth into the work of reporters and media. Reveal wise paths to our President and all who are in office. As citizens, give us discernment, respect for governance, and a striving for what is good.*

   This week, move each of us to pray as we read or watch the news.
   We want to be agents of RIGHTEOUSNESS in your kingdom.

- *Please motivate all to respect the laws of this land and to work to change what is not fair, what does not protect, what is not just. Protect law enforcers, military, and first responders, so that they may be calm and wise in the midst of upheaval and violence.*

  This week, call each of us to account for the little ways we slither around rules. Lead us into obedience. We want to be agents of ORDER in your kingdom.

Holy Spirit*, please be present in the activities of this church so that through our ministries You are glorified.*
(Church events mentioned.)

Lord Jesus*, we need you every hour. Thank You for abiding with us in our struggles, decision-making, and joys.*
(Member needs mentioned.)

Triune God*, great is Your faithfulness.*
Thank you for listening to and answering our prayers.
This week, move us to be agents of PRAYER.

We love you. We praise you.

In the powerful Name of Jesus our Lord,

Amen.

REMEMBERING PALM SUNDAY

We exalt You, O LORD, and praise Your name,
for in perfect faithfulness you have done marvelous things.
The prophet Isaiah [9:6] said that You would be called
"Wonderful Counselor, Mighty God, Everlasting Father, Prince of
Peace" . . . that you would establish Your kingdom with justice and
righteousness forever.

Because You are our King, this morning we lay before You
*the **desires and worries** of our hearts.* [needs of the group]
Please whisper peace to us.

*King Jesus, **our country** struggles with violence,*
and marches for various definitions of justice.
We remember that as you entered Jerusalem,
You wept over the city because of her obstinacy and sin.
Yet, you rode in through the Sheep Gate, turning your face toward
your crucifixion, willing to be the Lamb slain for us.
Thank you, Jesus,
Please have mercy on our country.

Lord Jesus, as You humbly entered Jerusalem,
*crowds of adults and **children** triumphantly shouted,[Mt. 21:9]*
"Hosanna to [Him]. . . who comes in the name of the LORD!"
You told Your adversaries that from the lips of children
You ordained praise. [Mt. 21:16]
Thank You for the youth of this congregation.
Please protect their bodies and their hearts.
Strengthen our resolve to train them in Your ways.

*Please shape us into a captivating **community of faith***
that models trust, obedient service, and joy in You.
Humble our hearts this Passion Week.
*Inspire us to be **people of the Word and people of prayer***
who daily lay before you our friends and neighbors
and the events of our news broadcasts.
Give us courage to testify of Your will.
Give us wisdom and compassion to act
*as **agents of Your kingdom** rather than products of our culture.*

May we make known among the nations
Your Name and renown, Your justice and righteousness.

*Holy God, the Bible teaches us to **praise and worship You.***
Thank You for Pastor's faithful preaching.
Bless his teaching this morning.
Thank you for providing your church with hymns and Psalms,
for creating instruments and training musicians.
Thank you for the leadership of (named music staff),
for the organists and instrumentalists within our church,
for the choir you have provided,
and for the joyful noise of our congregation.
May we ever sing to You, Lord, for You have done glorious things!
Lord God Almighty,
You are always with us, never leaving us alone.
We love You, Lord.

Hosanna! Blessed are You, our covenant God and King!

In Jesus' name we pray,

Amen.

TEMPLATE: INCORPORATING SCRIPTURE

Excerpts from a prayer by **Chris Poley**.

We come to You this morning,
Holy God—Father, Son, and Holy Ghost—in awe of who You are.
You, Lord, are the Maker of all good things.
Everything You make is perfect and enduring.
Ecclesiastes[3:14] says, "Everything God does will endure forever;
nothing can be added to it and nothing taken from it."
Your power, Lord, is unfathomable to us.

Job 26[7- 8a, 10, 12a, 13a, 14a]speaks of You, Lord:

> *He spreads out the northern skies over empty space;*
> *he suspends the earth over nothing.*
> *He wraps up the waters in his clouds . . . .*
> *He marks out the horizon on the face of the waters*
> *for a boundary between light and darkness . . . .*
> *By his power he churned up the sea . . . .*
> *By his breath the skies became fair . . . .*
> *And these are but the outer fringe of his works;*
> *how faint the whisper we hear of him!*

Lord, it is impossible for us to understand
why an omnipotent, omnipresent, omniscient,
"Holy, holy, holy" God spends even a micro-second loving us.
And yet, Lord, Your promise to Abraham [Gen. 17:7]was:

> *I will establish my covenant as an everlasting covenant*
> *between me and you and your descendants after you*
> *for the generations to come, to be your God and the God*
> *of your descendants after you.*

Lord, You love us in ways that we don't fully understand.
You are always faithful, always true, and always with us.
You carry us every day,
even on those days when we are arrogant,
believing we can walk this world without You.

Lord, we pray to You, as did the author of Psalm 25:5,
to to help us on those arrogant days:

Show me your ways, Lord, / teach me your paths.
Guide me in your truth and teach me,
for you are God my Savior,
and my hope is in you all day long.

Evidence of that hope is all around us, Lord.
We look back and see your hand upon our church and upon our lives.
Holy Spirit, you have moved us in ways that we could not do on our own . . . (listed items).

Father, Son, and Holy Spirit, help us to humble ourselves before you, walking the path that you have laid out before us, and away from the path of evil. We humbly ask that You bless us in the coming year as we seek Your will. (Requests for staff, ministries, groups)

We ask that the Holy Spirit awaken us, that we seek You first.
When we arise in the morning, Holy Spirit, prompt us to prayer.
When we take our steps during the day, fix our minds on love and grace. As it says in Hebrews 18:13:

> *Let us hold unswervingly to the hope we profess, for he who promised is faithful. And let us consider how we may spur one another on toward love and good deeds.*

When we sit in the evening, draw us to Your holy Word,
and when we lie down to rest, send us back to prayer again.
Thank You, Lord, for giving us the gift of prayer.
Thank you for listening as we cry out to You.

Thank You, Lord, for hearing this prayer.

Amen.

TEMPLATE: TRINITARIAN EASTER PRAYER
by **Ron VanderMolen**

God the Father,

We approach you because You are our God and we are Your people.
Please accept our adoration, thanks, and petitions.
We come to You at this Easter time to celebrate
Jesus' resurrection—please give us joy.
We come with special fear because of
worldwide anxiety and death—please calm us.
We come at a time of great illness—please heal the sick.
We come at a time of great economic loss—
please give all people security.
You have been Your people's Rock of Salvation
throughout the ages.
In this time of great fear, insecurity, and even doubt,
may we know that You are with us.
May we follow Jesus Christ's vision:
You are our God, and You only will we serve.

**Heavenly Father, as you did with Old Testament prophets, and saints
ever since, please give us meaningful faith.**

God the Son,

Today, as we celebrate Your resurrection,
may we not forget that You became
both a person like us and our Savior, as well.
You know our needs.
We know that You were born, raised, and experienced suffering,
just as Your children have throughout history—
may we appreciate Your humanity.
As our Savior, You felt abandoned,
but You continued to honor Your Father's will—
may we, as Job, do the same in this critical time.
Though You died, You rose again and defeated death—
may we trust Your power over death.
May we rely on You, Jesus Christ, as our Lord and Savior.

**Lord Jesus, as You did with Your apostles and with Your followers
ever since, please help us to live daily with great hope.**

God the Holy Spirit,

*We depend entirely on You
to lead and guide us in all our ways.
May Your Spirit-inspired Word be our infallible guide.
May Your Spirit-filled love guide us
as we deal with all our fellow humans.
May we be led by You
to share our faith with others by word and actions.*

**Holy Spirit, as you have throughout all ages, help us to love God
above all and to love our fellow humans as ourselves.**

*We pray fervently that we always will value
the historic Christian church;
that we will experience communion of the saints
in this church, especially in times like these;
that we will constantly desire to overcome evil in our lives;
and that we will always know that
we will join the Triune God with resurrected bodies in eternal life.*

*Dear God,
as we celebrate Jesus' resurrection today,
help us to live our faith, depend on our hope,
and demonstrate great love.
Let us always live as disciples of Christ our Lord
and as children of the Father, the Son, and the Holy Spirit.*

Amen.

Talking with the Trinity

EASTER

Lord,
You are risen! We exalt You!
Creator God, Resurrected Lord, life-giving Spirit Breath,
Victorious God of life, we praise You!
You have opened the way for us to unite with You!
Thank you for providing wholeness and joy in life—
food and exercise; work and leisure,
ministries and skills; learning, art, music, and beauty.
Thank you for relationships in which to practice love, forgiveness,
encouragement, and partnership.

Sometimes we choose what does not satisfy.
Sometimes we work in our own power.
Sometimes it feels as if life is being sucked out of us
by our continuing sins, idols, addictions, and worries.
Forgive us and refine us—even though it may be painful—
so that we shine for You.
Remind us that Your death can free us from all bondage.
Empower us by Your Spirit to live in victory.
Increase our faith, Lord.

Please use us to minister to the illnesses and weaknesses of others.
Give us courage to point to You to heal brokenness.
Open our hearts to Your Word's teachings and Your Spirit's leading,
Open our mouths to testify of Your Truth in our world.

Happy Easter, living LORD!
May you be glorified by saints and angels in heaven.
May You be glorified throughout the earth.
We love You. We worship You.

In Your Almighty and Living Name,

Amen.

HOW DO I LOVE MY NEIGHBOR?

Lord,

How should we be agents of love and justice?
We support agencies that house the homeless
and feed and clothe the poor.
We clean our bulging closets
and give our unwanted clothing to thrift stores.
We gather canned goods for drives and holiday sharing.
We contribute to Compassion Child, Bethany Christian Services,
and Operation Smile, helping children in foreign lands
to live life with more fullness and joy.

Yet we cringe at the proliferation
of tents and cardboard shanties along our streets.
We are angry about the number of people
who draw welfare and will not work.
We are overwhelmed by the influence of drugs
that leaves human beings to survive without sense.
We feel the need to protect ourselves
with guns, security cameras, beepers and pepper spray.
How is that "loving our neighbor"?

Help us to see your image in such neighbors.
You know about such living—fleeing as a refugee to Egypt,
giving up Your Glory to be raised in a house,
working in Joseph's construction shop,
walking the roads with no place to lay your head,
keeping company with a mostly civil gang of twelve and crowds.
How would you operate in times such as ours?

We know our hearts should love,
but our senses recoil and we keep our distance.
Have mercy, Lord, and teach us compassion and wisdom.

In Your name, we pray,

Amen.

FATHER'S DAY

Good morning, Father!

Thank you for this holy, happy, Lord's Day and Father's Day!

Abba, we cling to You because:
You create us and enter into covenant with us.
You welcome prodigals home with joyful open arms.
You adopt us as Your children through Jesus' blood.
You place us in Your family—this family—the Church.
You know what we need before we ask—and You provide.
You assure us, "In this world you will have trouble.
But take heart! I have overcome the world." [John 16:33]
You are the King of all history, placing rulers to fit Your purposes.
You bring good out of evil, even during pandemics and uprisings.

Glorify Your name in all the earth!

On this cultural holiday,
we give You thanks for the fathers who gave us life.
Thank You for the men shaped by your Word and Spirit to reflect You:
providing, mentoring, disciplining,
Whether biological fathers, adopted dads, step-dads,
grandfathers, or forefathers—we rejoice in their love and faith,
their humor and tears, their prayers for us.

LORD, in homes without fathers
or homes having fathers who don't reflect You,
we pray for protection and special care.
Call us all to You, as we all struggle with sin.
Open our hearts to follow Jesus, Your exact representation.
He said He is one with the Father;
He prayed to You, "Not my will, but Yours be done."[Luke 22:42]

*Father, You daily offer us **Your WORD**.*
May we choose to read it,
trusting Your wisdom over the politics and Facebook posts of our day.
Give us courage to be Kingdom people,
testifying to Your Truth and upholding Your law
to love God above all and our neighbors as ourselves.

Abba, You daily offer to us the pathway of **PRAYER.**
May we choose to bring all things to You,
trusting our access to Your power
when we seek Your will in Jesus Name.
Have mercy on our world.
We are floundering and fighting, getting sick and dying.
Save us from the enemy and strengthen our hope.

Father, You have placed **Your SPIRIT** *in our hearts.*
May we choose to **act** *as He leads,*
trusting **Your call** *to be servants in Your Kingdom.*
May we claim Your abundance
and overflow with Your love and righteousness.

Abba, whatever other concerns we have
for this day or the coming week—we lay them at Your feet.
We trust Your love.
May we do Your will.
May we honor you.

How we love you, Triune God!
You are the great I AM!

We pray these things in that name, which you gave to Jesus,

Amen.

TEMPLATE: LORD'S PRAYER (Mt. 6:9-13, bold)
by **Ron Vander Molen**

"Our Father in heaven, hallowed be Your name."

As Scripture says, "The Lord our God is One,
and Him only must we serve."
May we live lives which focus on You and Your will.

"Your kingdom come, Your will be done, on earth as it is in heaven."

May [the pastor's] *message today inspire us to understand what we*
must do to lead lives that are worthy of Your heavenly Kingdom.

Please help us to support organizations that promote kingdom causes:
institutions of Christian mercy,
Christian colleges and universities,
Calvin Seminary,
Christian schools—today we especially support
[our local Christian School] *with our offerings.*

When we face great evil or death,
and we question Your will,
comfort us with Your promises.

We especially ask that You comfort _____ *and his family*
in the death of [his wife]. *It has been a long difficult struggle for both;*
his dedication to her is a model for us all.

May we do Your will and submit to it, also.

"Give us today our daily bread."

May we experience the blessings of daily food
and the health to enjoy it.

We pray for those who seek good health, especially _____,
but also all those who have health concerns.
Please help us to provide daily bread to those who lack it,
especially those suffering refugees in Yemen, Syria,
and throughout Africa and South America.

"And forgive us our debts, as we also have forgiven our debtors."

*We pray that our guilt will be removed
by the grace of Christ, Who has paid our debt.*

Help us to reconcile with others, even those who have offended us.

*In these contentious days, may we promote reconciliation
in our personal relationships
and in political and religious matters, too.*

"And lead us not into temptation, but deliver us from evil one."

*We recognize our weakness in the face of the command
to love You above all
and to love our neighbors as we love ourselves.*

*May we find good direction and instruction in our church programs,
which help us and our children know how to covet what is good
and not yield to temptation.*

*Please deliver us from the temptations to serve other gods
and to take advantage of all those created in Your image.*

May evil hate be overcome by sacrificial love.

*We ask all these things
in the name of the Father, and the Son, and the Holy Spirit,
in the assurance that*
Yours is the Kingdom, the power, and the glory.

Amen.

Talking with the Trinity

BREATH (after a shooting)

Oh, Great God of Heaven,
occupy our hearts, our lives, our land.

Lord God, you are in control.
You allow evil, but You triumph over it.
You allow sin, but You died to save us from eternal damnation.
You created light, but you allow darkness.
You are the greatest and you are good.
There is no god greater,
there is no power greater,
there is no truth greater,
there is no love greater.
Father, Son, and Holy Spirit—
we worship You;
we trust in You;
our lives belong to You.

This morning we awoke to news reports of hate and death.
Bring calm into that situation, Lord.
Keep us from sensationalizing the evil actions of one person.
Give us patience to wait for all the facts.
Keep us from jumping into prejudice and fear.
Please move believers and people of good will to help there.
Please come close to the families that are mourning.

Great God, You speak a word, and we are created,
filled with the breath of life.
When You remove Your breath, we return to the dust.
Daily You fill us with the breath of your Spirit.
You can raise us from the dry bones of inaction
to become the living Body of Jesus Christ.
Breathing within us, You point us to the Word.
Speak to our hearts and move us to listen hour by hour.

Thank you for crossing human barriers to bring Your love.
You gave up Your glory to become human,
and reached out to the leper,
the tax collector,

the Gentiles,
the disdained women,
to all of us sinners.
May we never forget that we were created in Your image,
that our sin made a mess,
that You call us to become like You.
Give us courage to reach out to all people
with Your wisdom, love, compassion, and peace.
Help us to touch lives as You did
and bring hope and healing.
Please lead us into new paths of obedience and joy . . .

(current requests)

Breathe on [us], *Breath of God,*
Fill [us] *with life anew.*
That [we] *may love what Thou dost love*
and do what Thou wouldst do.
[Edwin Hatch, 1878 (https://hymnary.org/text/breathe_on_me_breath_of_god)]

In the Name of Jesus,

Amen.

Talking with the Trinity

PETITIONS WITH THANKSGIVING
by **John Schoolland**

Our Father in heaven,

*We are in awe when we think of **Who You Are!***
We join with David [Ps 19:1-2]when he says,

> *The heavens declare the glory of God; / the skies proclaim*
> *the work of his hands. / Day after day they pour forth speech; /*
> *night after night they display knowledge.*

We often take it for granted that one day follows the other and that the
seasons continue to change; but it only happens at Your command.

*We trust You for **supplying what we need.***
*You supply the **air** that we need for our breath, and **bodies** that turn*
food into energy. Our bodies are so complicated and we seldom think
about them until something stops working. Almost all of us have
*comfortable **places to live** and convenient methods of **transportation**;*
*the privilege of enjoying the **beauties of nature**—trees and mountains,*
the ocean, flowers and beautiful sunsets.

You are our Father and we are blessed to be your children.

*Our first parents were **tempted by the evil one.***
They failed the test; therefore, we have sin and misery amongst us.
We confess that we all too often listen to the one who tempted them.
Lord, we ask Your forgiveness.
When you were tempted, Lord, you were victorious.
Now we can live in that victory when we put our faith and trust in You.

*Help us, Lord, to remain strong in Your **Word and Spirit**.*
We thank you for your Word where we find
the way of life-everlasting and a guide to live by.

*Thank you **for this church home** where Your Word is taught and*
explained, and for the encouraging fellowship we enjoy.
*Thank You for our **Council**, who are conscientious in making necessary*
decisions, and are dedicated to caring for the people.
*Thank You for the **staff** that we have.*

May Pastor____ give us a positive response to be our senior pastor. Thank you for the many **volunteers** *who do their part in making our church a comfortable place to worship, learn, and have fellowship.*

We are thankful **for our free country** *where we can enjoy democracy instead of dictatorship. We are so blessed, but we realize that the evil one is at work, too. There are those in our land who want to forget you. Oh, Lord, we pray for them to be open to the clear evidence that things only exist by Your governing hand.*
We pray for our **leaders.** *Bless those who are Christians, that they may be a strong influence. We pray that You will open the hearts and minds of those who are not believers.*

We pray for **those who have lost loved ones** *recently and are missing them; fill that vacant place with your love and compassion. Awaken in us the reality that there is a wonderful future for each one of us who believes. There are* **those who are dealing with pain and health issues.** *Give wisdom to medical staff and bless what they are able to use for the relief and recovery of pain.*

Lord, we are looking forward to **the beginning of the season's activities.** *We thank you for the excitement in these preparations. We pray for a season of growing closer to You.*

Now we look forward to **what Pastor has prepared** *for us. Bless him with clarity of thought and speech.*

We ask it all in Jesus' name,

Amen.

TEMPLATE: PRAISE, THANKS, TRUST;
REFLECTING GOD'S CHARACTER
in all of our church's ministries and volunteers

Father, we praise You for creating, loving, and providing for us.
Thank You for exerting Your power to make life flourish and abound.

When we deal with health concerns, we trust that all the days planned
for us are written in Your book. We trust that You are able to restore
health, if it is Your will. (Needs mentioned)

Jesus, we praise You, for giving up Glory to live on earth and
experience our humanness, yet without sin. Thank you for Your
compassion, and for choosing the agony of the cross to save us.
Thank you for exerting Your power over death to rise from the grave
and ascend into heaven.

When our loved ones die, we trust that they are alive with You in Glory,
experiencing the joy of resurrection.

Holy Spirit, we praise You for giving us new life in Christ. Thank you
for purifying our prayers. Thank you for exerting Your power to
produce abundant fruit in our lives.

When we struggle to understand how to act as followers of Jesus,
we trust that You will bring His Word to mind and teach us how to be
lights in this world.

LORD GOD, You have called us into this church. As we close a church
calendar year, we thank You for providing this church with all the staff
and volunteers it has needed to be part of Your living, blessing Body.

You are the God of ORDER, putting leaders and workers in place.
Thank you for our faithful council. Thank you for the search team.
Thank you for the strong organization and direction of Pastor _____.
Thank you, too, for this campus and all who maintain it; staff and
volunteers to clean and prune, to run the office, to set up and take
down, to handle finances and website and communication. Thank you
for willing volunteers who surround our Sundays with order – van
drivers, ushers and parking lot guards, nursery attendants, operators of
sound and screens, creators of Power Points and DVDs, greeters and

librarians, and those who bring flowers and visuals that enhance the sanctuary.

You are the God Who SPEAKS, *calling us to devote ourselves to Your WORD. Thank you for the sermons of Pastor _____ and all visiting pastors. Thank you for preparing teachers who instruct us: the leaders of Children's Worship; __ and leaders of Journey and Crosswalk; Sunday School/catechism/VBS teachers; youth/GEMS/Cadet leaders; LIFE group and Bible study leaders. Thank you for inspiring volunteers to minister at the Gospel Mission and Windsor Care Home and on the Outreach Team. Thank you for using us to support missionaries locally and in Japan.*

You are the God who desires and deserves our PRAISE. *As you provided thousands of musicians for worship in your tabernacle and temple in the Old Testament, You have provided an abundance of worship leaders in our church: directors of music, the Worship Planning Team, organist, pianists, solo musicians, the orchestra, choirs of adults and children and hand bells, the Praise Teams and band, and members who read and pray. Thank you, Lord. Please inspire us.*

You are the God who delights in FOOD and FELLOWSHIP. *Thank you for all the volunteers on the Kitchen Team, the Helping Hands Team, the Fellowship Team, and those who organize and serve Sunday coffees. Be with us in our love and laughter.*

You are the God Who hugs us with CARE *like a hen taking her chicks under her wing. Thank you for PRAYER-ministry volunteers who express care through the Sunday Prayer Team, the Prayer Chain, and Prayer Matters. Thank you, too, for volunteers who keep us connected to each other through the Mailbox Ministry and the Lamplighter. May we always think of each other as family.*

You are the God who PROVIDES ABUNDANCE, *so we can reach out and share. Thank you for providing volunteers who help through the Master's Hands and the Food Give Away. Thank you for volunteer liaisons with agencies of care such as Bethany Christian Services, Bethany's House, Bethany Home, the Redwood Center, InterFaith, and The Salvation Army. Please bless Sierra Salem Christian Homes with our offerings received this morning.*

Talking with the Trinity

You are the God who CALLS *each one of us to come to worship; to sing; to show up for games, concerts, and fundraisers; to encourage each other with compliments, visits, meals, and phone calls; to bring offerings; to blanket everything with prayer. Each one, whatever our age or abilities, gives life to this church and makes it thrive through Your leading.*

Please reward and strengthen all these brothers and sisters in Christ so that we may continue to thrive. As you did with the Pentecost church, Holy Spirit, please add to our numbers. Refresh us. Fan the flames of our love and our zeal. We want to shine for Your glory, Lord God. Give us courage to testify that we belong to the Triune God, Who provides abundantly, saves with grace, and leads on to victory! We love you, Lord.

In the powerful Name of Jesus we pray,

Amen.

TEMPLATE: GOD'S AGENDA "RATHER THAN"

Creator of small and great;
Provider of sun, water, and food;
God become man to save us;
Victor over sin, death, and the evil one;
Almighty King reigning for good:

You desire intimate communion with us!

Please move us to give up our petty agendas to do your great works:

- *Raising our children with wisdom and counsel, rather than stuff*
- *Spending time with the needy, rather than time just with friends*
- *Working and voting for justice, rather than posting disparaging social media comments*
- *Spending for Your causes, rather than buying into our addictions*
- *Creating things of beauty and basking in wonder, rather than accumulating gadgets we'll forget tomorrow*
- *Reading your Word, rather than trusting TV pundits*
- *Praying unceasingly with loving praise for You and advocacy for others, rather than rehearsing requests for our needs which You have already supplied*

As a church,
prepare us to lead our community into healthy, heavenly ways.
May our leaders grow spiritually as they plan practically.
May we members shun church busyness
but be active in the work of the Kingdom.
May we all schedule times of solitude to talk and listen to You,
Great Lover of our Souls.

In Your Name we pray,

Amen.

CHURCH FAMILY
by **Sandra Mason**

Father God,

We stand in awe that we can call You both our Father and our God.
You—the Creator of everything, perfect in all that you do, Ruler of
all—call us Your children, adopting us to be Your own! We are a very
broken people, tainted by sin, but You, Father, reached down through
Your Son for us. We can't thank You enough!
Lord, help us to continue to grow and understand the greatness of Who
You are and the depth of Your love for us.

In this body of believers . . .
Many of us are facing silent challenges,
and, Lord, we ask for Your vast wisdom and peace—
there are those who are struggling for wisdom
on how to parent children through challenging situations;
marriages that every time they make an improvement,
find something new coming to knock them down;
others who are struggling with health choices or medical issues;
those who are giving so much of themselves
to care for a declining family member;
those who every day are reminded that a piece of their life that is
supposed to be there is gone.
We bear these heavy burdens daily.
Send your Holy Spirit, the ultimate Comforter and Source of wisdom,
into these pains and struggles, Lord.

We are also thankful for the answer to prayers
with the "yes" from Pastor _____ and his family.
We look forward to their coming with eager anticipation.
Lord, this change affects so many people.
We pray for the _____ family as they work through the details of a
move that also involves goodbyes. Guide them and the details
that need to fall into place.
Also, be with the church body they will be leaving behind.
Give them comfort and hope in this challenging time.
Lord, prepare our church body. Give us the patience and grace as we
wait for their arrival and work through the time of transitions.

We are so thankful for the children of this church body.
On Wednesday nights, we hear the beautiful buzz of excited children.
On Sundays, we see the exit of our Children's Worship and
Sunday school kids. We are so thankful for each and every one.

Give us opportunities to show them how important they are
and what it means to passionately serve and love our Heavenly Father.
Bless them as they spread out to different schools each day.
May they be witnesses wherever they are.

May we learn from them. You tell us that to enter the kingdom of
heaven we are to have faith like a little child.
They have something to teach us, Lord. Humble us to see it.

We also pray for Rehoboth Christian School. Lord, bless that school
and the work they are doing. Thank you for the opportunity we have to
give to their ministry today. Lord, use this offering in a mighty way.

We praise you, Lord, for the gift and privilege
of worshipping Your Holy name.
Continue to bless our worship that it may be honoring to You.
Lord, worship is all about You; we desire to honor You!
Open our hearts to hear your Word;
allow us to hear exactly what You want to teach us today.
Bless Pastor as he brings his message;
give him the words that we need to hear.
We are thankful for all the many pastors who have come
to share their hearts with our church body in this in-between time.

Father God, we love you so much and are humbled by the love you
have for us and the blessings you shower upon us.

It is in Jesus' name we pray,

Amen.

TEMPLATE: FORM-TRANSFORM-REFORM

Almighty God,

Thank You for FORMING us,
for creating each one of us unique:
differing bodies, varying cultures and ethnicities, ages and talents,
personalities and experiences, training and family history.
Not one the same—even twins are a bit different!
Thank You that we can form groups—families, marriages,
communities, school classes, church groups, work teams—
and have others who care for us, teach us, and influence us.
We could not exist alone.
But togetherness challenges us—we must learn to love, forgive,
compromise, encourage, and serve.
Though we often resist, thank You for the hard work of
community-building and for the joys it brings.

This morning we pray for our <u>church</u>:
- *Please strengthen each person who has health concerns, some facing more severe symptoms and greater issues. Please relieve and heal those dealing with cancer, with back and joint pain, with failing eyesight, and with walking difficulties.*
- *Please come close to our children with special needs. May all children feel safe, encouraged, successful in school, cared for by friends and family, claimed and loved by You.*
- *Please bless our outreach into the community— the Harvest Party on Halloween, providing a safe place for community kids to come for candy; the Bells concert, in support of The Salvation Army.*

We pray, too, for our <u>country</u>.
- *As election time is upon our communities, may local officials and school board members be chosen who will work for what is right and good.*
- *Please give wisdom to federal government officials; may they resist special interests and greed. May the needs of our people be met in healthy ways. May our influence in the world be exercised with a keen ear to the good of other countries.*

Thank you for TRANS-FORMING us
through the truth of your Word and Your Spirit.
Help us to put off the old man and put on the new.
Inspire us to give up fears, bad habits, idols, and ill feelings.
Shape us to be like Jesus.
We trust You, LORD, to show us the ways of the Father
so we can glorify Him as His children.

Thank you for RE-FORMING Your church.
Thank You for leaders and thinkers who urged Your church
to test its behaviors and confessions against the Bible,
for men and women willing to die for their beliefs.
Thank You that we can create new wineskins
as we better understand Your truths.
Thank You for calling us to kingdom ventures
that stretch our comfort.
Please forgive us when we dig in our heels
to keep from moving forward.
Please continue to surround us,
hedging us in from the attacks of the evil one.

We praise You for being our God who is alive
and on the move, with only good purposes.
We love You, Lord.

In Jesus' Name we pray,

Amen.

AFTER THE SUDDEN DEATH OF OUR PASTOR

Lord Jesus,
Sometimes we feel so small, so confused, so alone.
Our feelings, concerns, and questions are swirling inside.
Please gather us close and quiet us this morning;
remind us of Your love, and answer us with Your wisdom.
Holy Spirit, please breathe in us and fill us.

Lord God, You are worthy of worship.
We sit in this sanctuary this morning to worship.
Remind us that all over this town, all over this country,
people are gathering in churches.
All over the world, Christians are gathering—
some at the risk of their live—to praise Your name.
Even in heaven, the saints of all the ages are bowing down—
Bible people such as Abraham, Moses and David,
Church Fathers such as Augustine,
Reformers such as Luther and Calvin,
great preachers such as Wesley and Edwards,
great pastors such as Pastor ____,
our grandparents and parents,
even some of our children.
They are worshipping before your throne,
joining the angel hosts to sing:
"You are worthy, our Lord and God, to receive glory and honor and power" (Rev 4:11a). "Great and marvelous are Your deeds . . . . Just and true are Your ways, King of the nations" (Rev 15:3).
Move us to sing with them, Lord—all of us together
worshipping You, praising You, honoring You!

Creator Father,
Your glory *is so vast that our telescopes hint at more than 350 trillion galaxies!* **Your complexity** *is so intricate—You created more than 228 distinct muscles in a worm! Yet You have written our names on Your hand and know when each hair falls from our heads.*
We are important to You.

Lord Jesus, You are alive and reigning!
You have been reigning since before the world was created and You

will be reigning into eternity. The story is Yours; You have chosen to write our lives into it. Nothing on this tiny time-bound planet happens outside of Your control and plan.

Thank you for establishing a redeemed relationship with us.
Although we live on this earth, we are citizens of Your Kingdom—alive today because You desire it; but when we die—scooped up in Your eternal arms to live with You forever.

We praise You that we may claim this comfort and security, claim Your providence and purpose, claim Your just rule and surpassing wisdom!

Great God,
please help us to bring glory to You—
Inspire us to faithfully spend our time, attention, and efforts.
Bring health to our emotions of grief, loneliness, anger, fear.
Fill our week with trust, hope, and joy.
Relieve our confusion—our frustration, doubts,
lack of knowledge, and loss of direction.
Strengthen our relationships with family, friends, and church.
Use us to meet the needs of which we know,
and to pray for the needs we can only guess at.
Please give hopeful direction in our future —may we have fulfilling work and safe homes; may You answer our questions about what You will be doing in this church and in the world.

Thank You. Lord, for Your grace and goodness!
Thank You for Your promises!
Thank You that in our weakness, You are strong.

We love You, Lord.
Thank You for hearing us in Jesus' name.
Amen.

Talking with the Trinity

CONFESSION and ASSURANCE

Good morning, Father.
Thank you for blossoms and rain and food and clothes
and church facilities and each other.
Holy Spirit, you have gathered us.
Our reasons for coming here are various: curiosity or leadership or
parents' expectations or habit or superstition or duty.
Turn our focus from all of these
to seek the welcoming arms of our forgiving Father.

We've just read Your Law
and claimed that we'll act with good behavior,
*but many of us didn't try to find **our** sins embedded there —*
sins we left at home or sins we are sinning now such as
pride, resentment, anger, apathy, abuse,
seeking esteem from other sources, buying into the lies of
advertising and the evil one that we're not good enough.
Holy Spirit, please rise up in us now.
Shine Your light into our darkest corners.
Take us to the cross.
Remind us of what Jesus did there for us.
Strip off our recurring sins and failures.
Clothe us in His righteousness.

Father, thank You for Your unconditional, never-ending love.
Gather us close. Quiet us with Your amazing grace.
Tell us over and over
> *that we were chosen before the world was created,*
> *that our names are etched on the palm of Your hand,*
> *that we are Your beloved children,*
> *that You will not remember our confessed sins,*
> *that You will protect us from the evil one,*
> *that we will live with You for all eternity.*
Remind us that Your Spirit lives within us,
renewing us and giving us Your power.

Teach us to reflect You, delivering compassion, not judgment.
Turn us around to see our world through Your eyes;
Send us out with our arms open wide in Your name,

welcoming, loving, restoring,
bringing others in to celebrate the Kingdom.

Today we remember before Your throne:
our children —
> *growing in the womb,*
> *readying to profess their faith,*
> *living away,*
> *serving in the military,*
> *wandering away;*

We remember the ill and grieving;
those facing persecution and death;
our missionaries;
our leaders;
Please be their Hope, their Guide, their Life, their Peace.

Thank You for Your abundance.
Give us discernment and wisdom to use Your resources well,
trusting that when we meet needs in Your name,
there is always enough.

Thank You for this worship celebration.
Thank You for this feast of Your Word through Pastor's message.

We love You, Father, Son, and Holy Spirit!

We pray this all in the power of Jesus' Name,

Amen.

TEMPLATE: YOU ARE . . . BUT WE . . .
by **Ron VanderMolen**

O God,

We turn to you as a Single Spiritual Being.
We call you God. We call you Father.
We give You our thanks and we ask for Your help.

Thank You for creating us in Your image,
but we fail to measure up to Your expectations.
Please help us become what You intended us to be.

You are eternal, but we are time-bound.
Please help us to see beyond our present troubles and anxieties.

You are unchangeable, but we chase after social fads.
Please help us to have truly godly, timeless values.

You are completely wise, but we tend toward ignorance.
Please help us to pursue the truth revealed in Your Word and nature.

You are just, but we trade justice for personal gain.
Please help us to work for individual and social justice.

You are good, but we tend toward selfishness.
Please help us to love without economic, social, and racial prejudice.

As we seek the welfare of others, please give Your comfort and
blessings to people who are close to us:
(needs of group)

In the name of the Father and the Son and the Holy Spirit,

Amen.

CHURCH (70ᵗʰ) ANNIVERSARY

Our Father in Heaven,

We praise You because You are the only true God,
guiding time forward toward Your appointed end.
Thank You for creating us and choosing us to be Your children.
Thank you, Lord Jesus, for dying on the cross for our sins,
for rising from the dead to reign forever.
Thank you, Holy Spirit, for calling us to faith,
for giving men and women vision and courage to follow You.

Thank you, Father, for raising up the Christian Reformed Church
and the worldwide ministries they have accomplished in Your name.
Thank You for establishing this church,
and for leading each of us to make this church our home.
Thank You for all of the leaders and pastors You have called to
minister here throughout these seventy years.
Thank You for Pastor _____'s ministry with us. Bless him,
our council, staff, and all teams as they seek to lead this church.

Thank You for each adult and child in this membership.
We rejoice that a number of the charter members
are still worshipping with us.
Thank You for creating family trees of covenantal faithfulness.
Please keep our children close to You,
and call them back if they wander.
Thank You for the ways You shape us,
teaching us to love and forgive so that we are always able
to renew our relationships and move forward.
Thank You for the sure hope of eternal life with You
and the comfort of knowing that members who have died are with You.

Lord, You have gathered us week after week,
generation after generation.
Although this anniversary is a great milestone to us,
to You it is just a blink. To You, 1000 years are but a day!
*Yet, our days **are** part of Your plan. May we spend them—*
faithful to Your Word and obedient to Your Spirit.
Please forgive us for times when we have sought our own purposes,

153

or have been arrogant about our beliefs and our history.
Forgive us if we have gloried in buildings or programs.
Forgive us if we have begun a task before we have prayed.
Forgive us if we have hoarded or refused to become involved.
Forgive us if we have hesitated to move out in faith.

*Lord, these years have been good because of **You**.*
You could have accomplished everything without us,
*but You chose to partner with us – You **in** us and we **in** you.*
***You** unleash Your powerful Word to others*
*through **our** teaching, preaching, and missionary work.*
***You** bless us abundantly, so that **we** are able to help the needy*
through our offerings and volunteer work.
***You** provide us with time, instruments, equipment, materials,*
*organizational skills, and voices, so that **we** can be creative.*
***You** use **our** prayers to heal the difficult and unhealthy*
conditions of our lives.
***We** are humbled to be **Your** children, **Your** servants.*

Lord Jesus, anniversaries look back, but time moves on;
the world and our culture continue to change. Yet, in Your Word,
You said to the patriarchs, to the disciples, and to us:

> *"Fill the earth and subdue it. Rule over [it]" [Gen. 1:28b].*
> *"I will bless you . . . and you will be a blessing" [Gen. 12:2].*
> *"So you will be my people, and I will be your God" [Jer. 30:22].*
> *"Love the Lord your God . . . . love your neighbor as yourself"*
> *[Mt. 22:37-39].*
> *"Be strong and courageous. Do not be terrified; do not be*
> *discouraged . . ." [Josh. 1:9].*
> *"Go and make disciples of all nations, baptizing them in the name*
> *of the Father and of the Son and of the Holy Spirit, and teaching*
> *them to obey everything I have commanded you. And surely I am*
> *with you always, to the very end of the age" [Mt. 28:19-20].*

Father, today call our hearts to renew our covenant to serve You.
May we follow You into the future,
knowing You will be with us;
knowing You never fail;
knowing You have won the victory over the evil one, death, and hell.

May Your Name be exalted!
May Your Kingdom come!
May this church continue to grow into Christ our Head.
May this city be blessed, because we are working in it for You.
May we have years – and eternity—to serve and praise You!
We love You, Almighty God, Lord Jesus, Holy Spirit.
We praise You!

In Jesus' Name,

Amen.

Talking with the Trinity

THANKSGIVING

Good morning, Father, Son, and Holy Spirit!

We bring to you our praise and thanksgiving,
even though this Covid year has closed us in.
We feel its restrictions today,
as worship is online and family gatherings are pared down.
Thank You for all the efforts made to keep us safe and healthy.
Please lift our spirits to remember that:

> *This is [our] Father's world;*
> *and to [our] listening ears*
> *all nature sings and round [us] rings*
> *the music of the spheres.*
> [Maltbie D. Babcock, 1901
> (https://hymnary.org/text/this_is_my_fathers_world_and_to_my)]

May we receive and delight in ALL that is outside our doorsteps,
in the pictures on our computers, in the memories of our travels.

You are the Three-in-One God—
***varied** in Your workings yet unified in Your purposes.*
*Your creation reflects You in its awesome **diversity**!*
*You have created mind-boggling **variety and color**,*
taking our breath away with simple beauty and magnificent splendor!

This morning we cannot possibly detail
the expanses of the universe with its galaxies and planets;
the soils, rocks, and waters of the earth;
the kingdoms of all living things... but we can try!

Thank You for...

- *The shade TREES, CACTI and BUSHES—mixed together in height, shape, leaf type and color—Chinese pistachio, ginko, redwoods, and more!*
- *Your FLOWERS in the wild and in our gardens—poppies, lupine, tulips, and more!*
- *Your GRAINS and FIBERS for fabrics and food—cotton, flax, wheat, corn, and more!*

- *Acres of VEGETABLES and VEGETABLE FRUITS—lettuce, beans, tomatoes, pumpkins, and more!*
- *Bins of FRUITS—strawberries, oranges, lemons, grapes, and more!*
- *Truckloads of NUTS—almonds, pecans, walnuts, and more!*
- *Wild ANIMALS and REPTILES that roam—coyote, buffalo, giraffes, alligators, lizards, and more!*
- *HERDS in the pastures—cows, sheep, pigs, horses, and more!*
- *FISH and SHELL FISH in Your waters—salmon, lobster, clams, and more!*
- *Wild and domesticated BIRDS—bluebirds, canaries, cardinals, seagulls, eagles, hummingbirds, turkeys, and more!*
- *Your winged and walking INSECTS—ladybugs, flies, ants, spiders, and more!*
- *And all our precious PETS—dogs, cats, turtles, parakeets, and more!*

The whole world is in Your hands,
needing Your care and Your provision
of sun and water, land and sustenance.

And so, too, Your PEOPLE—
People of all races and ethnicities, natives and immigrants,
in families, neighborhoods, cities, our country, our world!

People to whom You have given the breath of life,
for whom You have died,
and within whom You are willing to live.

Thank you, LORD God, for creating out of Your love
and giving to each of us
thoughts, emotions, and the ability to communicate,
*so that we are able to reflect Your **creative power**,*
*and be a **blessing** in all areas of our life.*

Thank You for homeschooling us all this year
so that we could learn Your lessons of new ways
to work and communicate, play and worship.

Thank you that in the truth of Your Word we may learn
how to love our neighbors and worship You.
Thank you for rising from the grave
and making us resurrection people,

Talking with the Trinity

who—even in the midst of a pandemic—
even when hardship and grief come our way—
can testify with confidence
that peace, hope, and joy are available in You.

*May we proclaim that God is **great** and God is **good**.*
*May we **thank** Him for all He has given.*
May we be people who, even in quarantine,
hold up Your world in PRAYER.

Thank You, precious Trinity, for Your love and Your grace.
We love you, LORD.
May Your holy Name receive all honor and glory!

In Your name we pray,

Amen.

GOD OF ALL PEOPLE

Precious Triune God,

We praise You for Your goodness.
We thank You for calling us into Your community
ruled by our victorious Lord Jesus Christ.
We don't want to live away from You or outside of Your will.

You have created all life. You open and close wombs.
You create us in Your image.
Please forgive us for hatred and racism,
for fear and hostility toward others.
May we look with delight into the eyes
of each person of every color and creed—
May we see the person You created,
the person You want to draw near to You.
Remind us that, but for Your grace,
we would be "Gentiles" apart from You.
Thank you that Your Spirit called to us
and now we are Your children, too.

*Please make us eager to **act** in Your kingdom*
for Your glory, not our ease.
Take us to where Your Spirit is working as active yeast.
Ready us to work and to speak for You—
in this community, on our jobs, within our families.
Whatever this next week brings,
we trust that You will lead us,
holding us in the adventure, the joys, the battles.

Spirit, open our ears now, so we hear You speak.
Open our eyes, so that we see Jesus.
Fill us, so our hearts are strengthened to follow our Lord.

In Jesus' Name,

Amen.

Talking with the Trinity

HOPE—First week of ADVENT

Good morning, Lord God!

You are our King—almighty, sure, and good—
the only God, reigning forever.
We praise You for Your care and Your provision.
We praise You for the rain and snowpack,
for stopping the fires, for the spectacular display of changing colors,
for this Advent season.

Much as we delight in these things,
they also remind us of the seemingly unsteady, changing,
shifting circumstances of our lives.
We despair over the loss of people and property in fires,
we shake our heads at the mess of mudslides,
we cringe over the slippery conditions of ice and piling snow,
we recognize death in the falling leaves,
we bemoan the swift passing of another year.
We are a people prone to weak wishing,
rather than trusting and praying.
Help us to know that You are our secure HOPE,
our sure foundation, our anchor, our solid rock.

From the beginning, You created us as Your children,
giving us hearts to love and praise You.
You entered into faithful-forever covenant with us.
You provided a written record of Your good and mighty acts,
a Bible that reveals the truth and goodness
of Your plans, purposes, and promises.

Jesus, You came to earth to teach us how to live
and show us how to serve.
You died and rose victorious,
securing our salvation and our eternal life.
You ascended as Mighty Conqueror over the accuser, sin, and death.
Because of You, life can be restored.
Because of You, we eagerly await the future.
You have gifted us with Your Spirit to point us to truth
and lead us with sure steps in Your ways.

You have given us this avenue of prayer.
Thank you for listening, for assuring us that You will answer.

As your HOPEFUL gathered people, we bring You these concerns:

- *Please bring relief to our broken world, suffering with wars and hatred, disasters and disease, abuse and addictions. Use us to provide security and help through our prayers and generosity.*
- *Please give strength and wisdom to our leaders, that the needs of all may be met with dignity. Comfort the nation as we mourn the death of President Bush. Thank you for his leadership.*
- *Please give confidence to those who are aging and unable to worship with us. Use us to acknowledge them and to bring them joy.*
- *Please bless The Giving Tree event and all programs designed to provide for needy families this season. May our generosity of food and presents lead families to praise and worship You as the Giver of all good gifts.*

Thank you for this season of Advent, a time to worship
and rejoice in Your gift of Immanuel—God WITH us!
How we love You, LORD! Please lead us this week.

In the Name of Jesus,

Amen.

TEMPLATE: THE WAY, THE TRUTH, THE LIFE

LORD God, You are "the WAY, the TRUTH, and the LIFE"!
[John 14:6]

*Thank You for Your good and almighty **ways**:*
creating, providing, and sustaining all,
controlling the forces of nature that at times, overwhelm us—
winds, avalanches, earthquakes, floods, and fires.

*Thank You for revealing Your **truth** to us*
in Your glorious creation,
in Your Word,
through Your Spirit,
and through the fellowship of believers.

*Thank you for breathing **life** into us—*
nurturing us with the blessings of Your abundance,
resurrecting us from sin and evil and death.

Lord God—there is no other like You!
We praise You! We love You!

*As **children of Adam**, tainted with sin,*

* *we are culpable for the **ways** of this world.*
* *We struggle with **truth** and integrity, honor, and brotherly love.*
* *We ache for **life** lost through wars, persecutions, martyrdom, assassinations and murders, abortion, suicide, addictions, natural disasters, illness, and aging.*

*Holy Spirit, please assure our hearts that we have been saved and restored to be **children of God**, created in His image.*

* *Open us to God's **ways** of love through Jesus.*
* *Open us to the **truth** of the Bible.*
* *Open us to prayerfully produce the fruits of abundant **life**.*
 Holy Trinity, we long for abundant life with you.

*We bring before you **our children**.*
* *Please call their hearts to Your **ways***
  and protect them from evil.

* *May the **truth** of Your Word and Spirit*
  *and the examples of our lives invite them to **live** with You,*
  talk with You, delight in Your world,
  and dedicate their lives to serve You.

*We bring before You **our elderly**.*
* *Please help them navigate the **ways** and weaknesses of aging.*
* *May the **truth** of Your Word and Spirit*
  and our presence, cards, and visits,
  *assure them that their **lives** have influence,*
  that they are not alone, that You hear their prayers.
  We bring before you... (further needs)

Almighty God, be glorified in us
* *as we actively carry on Jesus' **ways** of restoration;*
* *as we testify to Father's **truth;***
* *as we nurture the Spirit's **life** in all of creation.*

Father, Son, and Holy Spirit,
glorify Your Name in all the earth!

Amen.

Talking with the Trinity

RESCUE

Good morning, Lord God!

Thank you for calling us to be Your children and Your church.
Thank you for saving us, for washing us clean in Jesus' blood,
for sending Your Spirit to guide us in our living.

Most of us, if not all of us,
have spent this week trying to live as Your Kingdom people.
We have found comfort and joy
in receiving the power of Your Spirit,
in reading Your Word for direction and truth,
in knowing that our prayers are heard in Your throne room!

Please forgive us if this week
we tried to live on our own apart from You.
Please rescue us. Help us reconsider and return to You.

Sometimes, Lord, it feels overwhelming to be just a little church
in the midst of brokenness and decay.
We sense that the evil one and his buddies are just around the corner,
gleefully bullying people, tempting us,
and trying to trip up the whole world.

We know, King Jesus,
that You already have the victory over Satan and his hosts:
they are dying, they are withering, they are having their last hurrah.
Please protect us and inspire us with courage
to bring hope to those who are struggling.
Long ago, you rested Noah's ark on the top of a mountain.
You divided swirling water several times
to bring Israel and your tabernacle through on dry ground.
You reached down into muddy pits
to save David and Hezekiah and Joseph.
You said, "Quiet! Be still!" [Mk.4:39] and calmed the Sea of Galilee,
protecting the disciples in their little boat.
We trust that You will lead us and rescue us
from all that threatens to drown us and wash us away—
confessed bad choices, health struggles, losses, and death.
You are our rock. You are our God in Whom we trust.

Please lead us into faith-filled interactions
with people outside this church.
We ask for Your blessing on the new City Access Center,
the expanded Shelter, as well as the Gospel Mission
as they all reach out to rescue homeless clients.
Lead us into loving conversations and deep listening
with those who are like us and those who are different from us,
such as our Food Give Away clients
and the families at the Giving Tree gathering.
May we be a community
in which all are known, loved, and cared for.

Please lead our country
to high purpose and honorable governance.
Holding to Your standards, may we be a nation of peace.

> *Lead on, O King Eternal,*
> *We follow, not with fears,*
> *For gladness breaks like morning*
> *Where're Your face appears.*
> [Ernest W. Shurtleff, 1887
> (https://hymnary.org/text/lead_on_o_king_eternal_the_day_of_march)]

We love you Lord and we pray this in Your powerful name,

Amen.

END OF THE YEAR
by **Dave and Babs Veneman**

We praise you, Almighty Trinity!

You are Father, Son, and Holy Spirit.
You alone are sovereign;
King over all kings and Ruler over all nations of the earth.
You alone are all-seeing and all-knowing.
You alone are righteous.
You alone are worthy of all glory and honor and praise.
You have made Yourself known to Your people through the Holy Spirit.
You do not change;
You are the God Who brought Your people out of bondage
in the Old Testament, and through the work of Your Son,
You still release people from bondage today.
Your will, God, is good and perfect.
Your ways are flawless.
Your judgments are upright.
Your Word is without error.

We thank you, Jesus,
for interceding before the Father to declare us righteous.
Thank you for welcoming us to approach the throne of grace.
Thank you for Your daily Presence through the Holy Spirit.

*Lord, we pray for **our local church** this morning.*
Thank you for the leadership of our pastors and council.
Thank you for the many people who faithfully lead
Bible studies and youth programs.
May the Spirit bring power to their words as they give out the gospel.
Help us to learn from the faith of our spiritual leaders
and to joyfully encourage them.

*Lord, we pray for the **members of our congregation***
who are lonely, or sad, or frustrated, or anxious.
God, You are merciful and loving.
You know the heartaches and confusion of every soul.
You have promised to be with us always.
Please send Your Spirit to comfort, to convict, to direct,

or to encourage as each personal need requires.
Please fill all our hearts with hope and with joy
that surpasses the world's understanding.

*We pray for our **nation's local, state, and federal leaders.***
Please give them wisdom and a strong sense of justice.
May each have a servant's heart,
desiring to do his or her job with integrity and honesty,
putting the good of the nation above personal gain and agenda.

*Father, we pray for a spiritual **revival across our nation.***
May people turn their hearts toward Your Son,
and may a spirit of repentance come upon our land.
May many new members be added to Your Kingdom,
and may solid Bible-believing churches experience growth.

*Lord, we pray for those in the **global Church***
who are right now suffering
for simply loving You and choosing to live godly lives.
Help them to not be afraid and to remain alert in prayer,
relying on Your power for strength and courage.
Please give them peace and hope.

God, we know that You are more powerful
than any evil or darkness in the world.
Even though it may seem impossible at times, we know that You alone
can flood even the darkest heart with Your Light,
and so, we pray that those who are actively fighting against
Your Church, will someday have an encounter with Jesus.
May they have a total heart change!
Father, please allow the persecutors to come to know Jesus
as the Lord and Savior of their lives.

Lord, as we are looking toward a new year,
please help us to think about our days wisely.
Help us to consider how You would have us
spend the time You have given us.
Enable us to serve well, and with good cheer.
Give us open eyes to see opportunities to help others;
give us willing hands to work,

Talking with the Trinity

*and give us eagerness and clarity as we tell family, friends, and
neighbors about Your great offer of salvation.
Help us to be willing to invest time into others
for the glory of Your Name.
In this new year, Lord, help us to be bold witnesses for You.*

*Almighty God, thank you for loving us.
Thank you for being with us always.
Thank you for hearing our prayer this morning.*

*We pray all these things in the Name of the One who is
Wonderful Counselor,
Mighty God,
Everlasting Father,
the Prince of Peace.*[Is. 9:6]

Amen.

FOR THE PERSECUTED CHURCH

Thank You, Father,
for the gift of belief in Jesus Christ
and for calling us into the Kingdom of Your will.
Thank You that You are only good, and that You have sovereign power.

We pray for your Church which spans the globe.
Although believers praise You,
every day they wrestle with the evil one, the world,
and all forms of rebellion against Your will.
Because they claim the Name of Jesus,
believers experience threats, exclusion, oppression, hatred, and death.
We praise You that Christ has already won the victory.
We praise you that even in places where it is persecuted,
Your church is growing with vigor and health.
We praise You that You never abandon Your children, Your Church.

Please safeguard Christians who dare to claim Your Name.
Thank you for clothing believers in Your armor of
salvation, righteousness, the Word of truth, faith, and peace.
Please supply believers with courage and patience
as they continue to stand.
May they know that they are not alone.
Enable them to keep the faith, fight the good fight,
and finish the race.

Holy Spirit, move our hearts to faithfully pray for oppressed believers.
Here in our town, please shape us by Your ways and Word
to respond with eager obedience.
Give us courage to approach and love others without prejudice.
Give us vision and wisdom to energetically follow Your lead,
to work to bring all areas of our activity and influence
under Your Lordship.
Please place us where we need to be
to speak Your truth and tell of You saving grace.
Please use our obedience
to light the way for others to come into Your Kingdom.
Equip us for the difficulties, resistance, and suffering
that may come our way as we walk with You.

Talking with the Trinity

Lord Jesus, no matter the cost,
we ask that Your Church will grow until it fills the earth
and everyone shouts:

> *Glory to the Lamb that was slain!*
> *Praise to the Christ who has overcome*
> *sin and Satan, death and hell!*
> *Glory to our victorious Lord who reigns forever!*

In the name of the great I AM we pray,

Amen.

THE CHURCH in the WORLD
by **Sandra Mason**

Father,

You are good.
We will sing to the Lord for He is highly exalted.
You are our strength and our song. You are our salvation.
The Lord is our God and we will praise Him.
Lord, You are a warrior—majestic in power and holiness,
awesome in glory, and working wonders.
You have given us an unfailing love and You are our guide.
In Your majesty and power, You reign forever and ever,
for You are highly exalted.

We need You.
As individuals and as a church body we need You.
We desire to be a church that shines the light of Jesus
in everything that we do.
As sinful humans we can't do this.
Please, Lord, fill every single piece of our lives with You.
Denying ourselves and fully surrendering to You
can be painful and hard.
So, Lord, please give us the strength to do this.
Help us to help each other to take an honest look at ourselves;
shine a light on the places of our hearts that need repentance.
Give us the strength to be real and honest
with ourselves and each other.
Then, Lord, give others a heart of love without judgment.
Everyone here has a different story, a different struggle;
meet them right where they are, Father.
For those who are lonely, be present with them;
help them cling to the promise
that You will never leave or forsake us.
For those who feel trapped, remind them of the promise
that You will always provide a way out.
Help them to look to You for that way out.
For those who are in physical pain, be their healer and comfort.
For those who are questioning if You are truly who You say You are,
lead them to truth, open their eyes to see You,

Talking with the Trinity

and give them safe places to ask questions.
For those who feel lost, remind them that You are
the way and the truth; guide them to truth.
For those who feel that no one would possibly be able to understand
the struggle they find themselves in,
remind them that You have experienced everything
and that You understand.
Lord, show them the right person to talk to
and give them strength to be honest.
Father, You established the church
to be a community that builds each other up,
that mourns with each other, and that celebrates with each other.
When we are being the church You called us to be,
no one should feel lonely; we need You to help us do this.
We want to be like the first church established in Acts.
Help us to be devoted to biblical teaching and to fellowship,
to the breaking of bread and to prayer.
Help us to be a church that works together, meets together,
and gives so that no one is in need.
May our church praise You and add numbers to Your kingdom!

The world needs You.
We don't have to look far to see the brokenness of the world.
Help the leaders of our nation, state, and city to have wisdom.
Lord, we ask that You bring people into leadership
that will be willing to boldly stand for You.
Give us wisdom about how to be a light in the dark world.
Protect us from the influences of the world.
Give us the boldness to say "no" and to remove
the things that negatively influence us from our lives.

Thank You! Thank You for Your truth and promises;
For the ways that You speak to us and show us who You are;
For the creation that speaks of Your glory and creativity;
For the Bible that is a guidebook for life.
Give us a hunger for Your Word.
Thank You for fellow believers who spur us on,
challenging us to grow, mourning with us in hurt,
and celebrating with us the work that You are doing.

*Thank You for the gift of prayer—that we can communicate with You
at any time, in any place, and for any reason.
Thank You that You loved us while we were yet sinners,
and took our sins on the cross, bearing our pain.
Thank You for this church, for the gifts You have given,
for the fellowship we can have, and for the hands and feet who serve.
Father, You have given us more than we will ever deserve.
We are so very grateful.
Help us to always have a heart of gratitude.*

In Jesus' name,

Amen.

NEW YEAR'S EVE 2020
by **Chris Poley**

I base this prayer on 1 Peter 1: 3-7:
"Praise be to the God and Father of our Lord Jesus Christ! In his great mercy he has given us new birth into a living hope through the resurrection of Jesus Christ from the dead, and into an inheritance that can never perish, spoil or fade. This inheritance is kept in heaven for you, who through faith are shielded by God's power until the coming of the salvation that is ready to be revealed in the last time. In all this you greatly rejoice, though now for a little while you may have had to suffer grief in all kinds of trials. These have come so that the proven genuineness of your faith—of greater worth than gold, which perishes even though refined by fire—may result in praise, glory and honor when Jesus Christ is revealed."

Our Father in heaven,
To say that we have had to "suffer grief in all kinds of trials" this year is an understatement. . . . In years past we have prayed for victims of wildfires, we have prayed for those who have suffered from devastating hurricanes and tornadoes, we have prayed when there have been riots and civil unrest, and we have prayed when criminals have chosen to blow things up for a cause. None of us knew that we would be on our knees praying for all of these things in one year, or that none of them would be the thing that defined this year . . . .

There has been much pain this year as we have longed to be together fully – talking without masks, standing close together, and offering handshakes and hugs. There has been pain at not being able to be at the bedsides of our brothers and sisters in Christ as they suffer illness or injury. There has been pain when we have needed or wanted to extend a shoulder to cry on, but instead had to talk over the phone. Lord, this year has also been very difficult when losing loved ones. Often there was no opportunity to share time together in remembrance of their lives. Even though we know they are with You in Glory, this hurt, Lord.

You know our hearts and You know our suffering. Your Word tells us that we will endure this, "for a little while." We confess, Lord, that our idea of "a little while" is closer to ten minutes than it is to a year or longer. We also confess that often we think that "proving the genuineness of our faith" ought not be this difficult. Forgive us, God, for not fully understanding and for not living life as the Apostle Peter writes in his epistle—that we should always be greatly rejoicing even when we are suffering.

*We don't know Your purposes, Lord, but we do know that You are sovereign and have a good reason for everything You do and everything You allow. Whatever Your plans for us individually, we can see that You are also working to get the attention of the lost. The number and intensity of the many calamities . . . serves to remind us that hope only comes from a resurrected Christ, and that if people turn their hearts to You, Lord, they will receive an inheritance in heaven that lasts forever. **Thanks be to God!***

Turn our hearts toward You so that we can rejoice in suffering and thereby bring "praise, glory and honor when Jesus Christ is revealed." This is our joy, Lord, and all we need, yet You give us so much more. You "shield us by your power." If with thankful hearts we look closely, we can see that this year was a time of great blessing, a time when You were faithful to us and provided more than we could have imagined.

- *When we think of our church body, thank You, Lord, for providing in Your providence two godly pastors during this difficult time. You knew that our needs would be greater this year and You gave us the spiritual leadership to fill those needs.*
- *Thank You for church staff who continued to work as to the Lord, blessing us with smiles and a willingness to adapt to the changes going on.*
- *Thank You, Lord, for giving us leadership in the area of worship as we adapted to changing requirements, sometimes on very short notice. What a blessing to have so many people come together to find a way to worship—through the internet and on the lawn!*
- *We also thank You, Lord, for providing for our budget needs. You have blessed Your people, who have then blessed this congregation, allowing us to meet our expenses and provide for needed computer equipment.*
- *Thank You, Lord, for bringing money into the benevolence fund. Many in our congregation have had financial struggles, requiring extra money to fill their needs. Thank You, Holy Spirit, for moving through the deacons, giving them compassionate and loving hearts and providing them wisdom.*
- *Thank You, Lord, for setting us on the road to evangelism with the Renewal Lab project. Thank You for the volunteers who are devoting*

themselves to showing us how we can grow as a church family. We pray that this will bring glory to You, Lord; that we can reach out to the community and share the good news of Jesus Christ.

- *We thank You, Lord, for blessing our church family with a baptism, several professions of faith, a marriage, and a birth.*
- *We thank You, Lord, for the blessings You have given us in our personal lives.*
- *Thank You for the ministry of those who went out of their way to create fellowship. Thank You for those who set up Zoom calls, sent cards or emails, or phoned just to say, "Hi."*
- *Thank You for the bountiful harvest we had this year. Thank You for the rain to help us with next year's harvest.*
- *Thank You for our employment and for employers that allowed us to work at home.*
- *We thank You for providing what we needed this year, even if it meant shopping online or asking a friend or family member to deliver.*
- *Thank You for all those who have been on the front lines with Covid-19, putting in extra hours to try to get us back to normal.*

While we have suffered with not being able to spend as much time with our loved ones as we would like, Lord, You have provided many of us with more time to spend with You. Thank You, Lord, for that extra time. Thank You for bringing us closer to You and making us more like Jesus. Thank You for giving each of us a heart to say what the Apostle Peter writes, "Praise be to the God and Father of our Lord Jesus Christ!"

In Jesus' name,

Amen.

APPENDIX

APPENDIX A
PRIVATE JOURNAL PRAYERS

In the introduction to this book, I mentioned that we sometimes *journal* our private conversations with God, using quite a different style than when we write public prayers. The three prayers below come from a journal I kept in 2015. Some readers might be interested to read three conversational journal prayers about the gift of healing. These prayers arose after I attended a seminar on healing at the CRC Prayer Summit and read Luke 4.

Lord, I believe You did these things. How do I translate these actions, this witness, into my own life and testimony? How I would love the gift of healing! It is beyond my understanding of all that is medicine and science, which are also good gifts from You, yes? Yet every day someone speaks of an ache or a pain. How blessed it must have been to come to You to be simply and authoritatively healed! But how exhausting for You as the word got out—people begging You to stay; long hours of healing. Thank You, Lord, for Your compassion and mercy! If this is to be part of my work, please prepare me from Your Word and curb my prideful nature to make me humble, not dramatic or focused on me.

***

Lord, as I explore the gift of healing prayer, I see that even life-long or enduring problems were immediately restored. I don't understand the faith to heal something like that—maybe a headache—but, wow! You can restore and heal immediately! I truly believe that. How do I become faith-filled to do so in Your name? I don't wish to "do magic" or say magic words/pious words outside Your will. I don't wish to build hope and then discourage. Were You to give me the gift of healing, would Your Spirit speak to my heart/brain so I would know if and when to proceed? Because, if things "didn't work" I know it would be because of me. I don't wish to "manipulate

Your power." I would love to bring people to faith in You. Is that arrogant . . . because You don't need any "help" with that? In Scripture, You avoided signs for the sake of signs. The motives were kingdom compassion and new life, not just healing. Didn't You heal faithful people after they were believers? Or was it only unbelievers to bring them to faith? Yet Lazarus was a believer. Please teach me to understand this gift. If it would make life and faith in You richer/deeper for others, I desire it. Is there a downside to a gift? Exhaustion? Crowds coming as You experienced? Teach me, Holy Spirit.

***

Re-reading Luke 6:19: "And the people all tried to touch him because power was coming from him and healing them all." Lord, it is as if You were a conduit of electricity, as if the whole Trinity poured forth from Your human-vessel presence. Could people see light and wind and "electricity"? They seemed to sense something more than just seeing the healings. Thank You for being such a beacon of good and restoration! May I trust You to be so when I pray to You for myself and others.

APPENDIX B
PRAYER STORIES

I shared the story of finding my car, a story in which I conversed with God in **doubt**. Below is an experience in which I conversed with God in **obedience.**

I was scheduled to speak at the Care Home for the Aging on Father's Day. I admit I was feeling lazy in my study of the Bible and I knew I had an old devotional talk in my files, so I pulled it and reworked it. As I went to bed on Saturday evening, I prayed, "Spirit, You know I have given this talk before. Please bring to mind anything about it that I should reconsider when I go over it in the morning."

I got up an hour early, ready to make any small changes the Spirit might have laid on my heart. However, the thought that came was, *Not this speech; talk on the Lord's Prayer about Our Father in heaven.*

"Lord, a whole new speech in one hour?! Hm . . . okay, okay. I have been teaching my Bible study on the Lord's Prayer, so I can do this, but what about a visual? I'm thinking that I should present the prayer petition by petition; it would be great to put them on the display board one at a time, but it's Sunday morning and I don't have any poster board to write on!"

Check your poster board box.

"No, Lord. I haven't bought any poster board recently. I don't have enough to do this!"

Check the poster board box.

I went into my study and knelt on the couch to peer over into the box behind the couch where I keep new poster board as well as the posters from previous speeches. Not expecting to see anything but used white poster board, I noticed three pieces of hot pink poster board. I pulled them out to find them fresh and clean. To this day, I have no memory of buying pink poster board, but there was just the amount I needed to write out the Lord's Prayer, petition by petition.

"Thank You, Lord!"

***

In the next two experiences, I conversed with God in **trust.**

My friends and I were leaving the theater in Sonora, CA. My friend Anna (94) was in the front seat and my colleague was in the back.

"Anna, shall we stop at the yarn store in Sonora that you like so well?"

"Sure!"

Immediately, I prayed out loud: "Lord, you know how crowded downtown Sonora can be. Anna would like to go to the yarn store, but we need a parking place right in front so that she can manage with her walker. Please give us that."

My colleague in the back chortled, "I would never pray like that!"

"Why not?" I countered. "God loves us, and He knows how Anna likes yarn. He can arrange that."

We drove another mile into the downtown area. Cars were moving at a snail's pace in both directions of the two-lane street. Every parking place along the street was full, yet when we reached the yarn store, amazingly, right in front of it was an empty parking space! We were on the other side of the road. We had to drive a block farther, wait to cut through the oncoming traffic, turn around, and head back, but when we got back to the yarn store, the parking space was still waiting for us.

"Thank you, Lord!"

***

My friend and I took a drive to the coast south of San Francisco. We stopped by Fort Funston hoping to see hang gliders and eat our picnic lunch, but there was no place to sit because workers were redoing the overlooking deck. So we got back into the car and headed south. I didn't know of any spot coming up that would afford us access to the ocean, but willy-nilly I turned into a residential area. As I did so, I prayed out loud, "Lord, I don't know this area, but we would like to enjoy Your ocean and eat our lunch. Is there a place here where we can do that?"

I drove to the last row of homes along the ocean, but there was no access. I turned right so that I was driving parallel with the ocean, but it was blocked by houses. After several blocks, ahead on our left we spotted a short extension of a cross street, evidently created to allow the residents in two ocean-front homes access to their side garages. This piece of street, only three-cars deep, ended in a chain-linked fence with a clear view out over the ocean.

We were able to park without infringing on anyone's property, so we got out, opened our lunch, leaned against the car and enjoyed the view!

"Thank You, Lord!"

APPENDIX C
BLOOD OATHS SEALING
GOD'S COVENANTS

When I was in seminary forty-five years ago, studying the Old Testament, my heart was captured by lectures on God's faithful dealings with and promises to His chosen people. What I am writing is based on my memory of those lectures; I no longer have the professor's notes. He spoke his own thoughts, but I recall that he also referenced a book titled *By Oath Consigned:A Reinterpretation of the Covenant Signs of Cirucumcision and Baptism* by Meridith Kline, Eerdmans, 1968. I believe this book is now out of print. I have always meant to read it, but so far have not, so I do not know if what I am writing reflects it.

***

In the beginning, God created mankind in His image and lovingly covenanted His eternal provision for them, giving them the Garden and fulfilling work.

> God blessed them and said to them, "Be fruitful and increase in number; fill the earth and subdue it. Rule over the fish in the sea and the birds in the sky and over every living creature that moves on the ground."
>
> (Gen. 1:28)

Father also set healthy boundaries for living in that Garden: You may eat of anything except the Tree of the Knowledge of Good and Evil. However, Adam and Eve broke covenant by eating of that tree. Overcome with guilt, they opened their eyes to realize that they were naked. Still loving them, the Giver of Life chose to sacrifice some of His animals—shedding their blood—so that He could cover the shame of Adam and Eve with skins. To save them from forever living in their sin, He additionally kicked them out of the Garden lest they eat of the Tree of Life.

The children of Adam and Eve multiplied and continued to sin rather than obey God. The holiness of Father could not tolerate this massive covenant disobedience, so He chose to destroy almost all humans and animals with a flood. Yet, with hope and love, He spared righteous Noah, his family, and the ark animals. When everything had been purged, He approached Noah with a covenant:

> I now establish my covenant with you and with your descendants after you and with . . . every living creature on earth. . . . . Never again will all life be destroyed by the waters of a flood; never again will there be a flood to destroy the earth.
>
> (Gen. 9:9-11)

Father placed a rainbow in the sky as a seal of His promise.

Because a *rainbow* is beautiful, we might forget that it portrays a piercing, blood-drawing weapon. Scholars believe Father chose it as the seal of His covenant. Like other Ancient Near Eastern malidictory blood oaths, it could be taken to mean that if the covenanter didn't keep his word, an arrow could be aimed at him to kill him. Of course, God can't be shot or killed, but Noah would have recognized in that sign how very serious Father was about His promise to never again destroy the earth.

Then Abraham entered history. Father chose him to be the father of His people, promising him a son and a family as vast as the stars in heaven and plenty of good land on which to live. He also told Abraham that it would be 400 years before all these promises were accomplished. There would be captivity and release from captivity before it was all over. Eager to get started, Abraham asked for a sign. Father told him to cut a heifer, a goat, and a ram in pieces, as well as to lay out some birds:

> When the sun had set and darkness had fallen, a smoking firepot with a blazing torch appeared and passed between the pieces. On that day the LORD made a covenant with Abram and said, "To your descendants I give this land."
>
> (Gen 15:17-18)

The miraculous passing of the firepot between the *cut and bleeding* animals, torching them, was like an ANE blood oath in which the covenanter pledged that if his promises didn't hold, he could be burned as were the cut animals. Of course, God can't be burned nor killed, but it showed Abraham how very serious God was about creating a great nation for Himself and giving them the Promised Land.

However, when Abraham was 99, the son who was needed to begin God's great nation had not yet been conceived. Abraham approached God about His covenant and Father assured Abraham that in His good time He would keep His promises. However, sensing

Abraham's distrust, He asked for Abraham's pledge of loyalty. Abraham and all males in his domain were to submit to God and wear a sign of faith (Rom. 4)—*circumcision*. Circumcision involved cutting and blood; it was a blood oath that carried the understanding that if the men broke trust with God, they might forfeit receiving His promises and die.

> Then God said to Abraham, "As for you, you must keep my covenant, you and your descendants after you for the generations to come . . . You are to undergo circumcision, and it will be the sign of the covenant between me and you. For the generations to come every male among you who is eight days old must be circumcised . . . . . My covenant in your flesh is to be an everlasting covenant .
>
> (Gen.17:9-14)

Every day, every circumcised Israelite man would see and be reminded of his very serious promise to belong to God Who would give him descendents upon descendents far into the future.

Just as Father had foretold, it was hundreds of years before the Israelites became a great nation in the land God had shown Abraham. First, they were taken captive into Egypt where they grew into a huge and ill-treated nation. Then, when the time was right, Father reached out in love to release them from captivity. The key to this release was a *reaffirmation* of Abraham's covenant. The terms of loyalty and promise had been spoken centuries earlier, but in full awareness, fresh promises of commitment needed to be made by the people with God. Father instructed them to take a *lamb* for each household, kill it, prepare its flesh for the Passover meal, and paint its blood on the doorposts of their houses.

> On that same night I will pass through Egypt and strike down every firstborn of both people and animals, and I will bring judgment on all the gods

of Egypt. I am the LORD. The blood will be a sign for
you on the houses where you are, and when I see the
blood, I will pass over you. No destructive plague
will touch you when I strike Egypt.

(Ex. 12: 12-13)

The Israelites knew that this covenant promised them
freedom, life, provision, protection, and leadership from God.
The *lamb's blood on the doorposts* was an oath sign meaning,
"If I do not trust in God and obey Him, may I die." It was a very
serious covenant.

Joyfully released from captivity, the Israelites headed toward the
Promised Land. Father gifted them with the Ten Commandments as
protective, healthy boundaries for good covenant living (Ex. 19: 4-6).
Further, Father commanded that these tablets of the law be placed in
the Ark of the Covenant, the "heart" of Father's traveling worship
center, the tabernacle. When they gathered at the tabernacle, the
Israelites acknowledged their relationship with Father by offering
incense prayers and bringing sacrifices of perfect, unblemished
animals to the priest, who slaughtered the animals and poured out
or sprinkled the blood on the altar. These *bloody sacrifices* sealed
their commitment to living in covenant holiness.

Moses took half of the blood and put it in bowls,
and the other half he splashed against the altar. Then
he took the Book of the Covenant and read it to the
people. They responded, "We will do everything the
LORD has said; we will obey." Moses then took the
blood, sprinkled it on the people and said, "This is
the blood of the covenant that the LORD has made
with you in accordance with all these words."

(Ex. 24: 6-8)

The sacrificed animals were a type of oath that carried the
meaning: "May these perfect animals take on the death penalty I

deserve, because the sins of my daily living threaten my covenant with Him, the holy God." The sheer amount of slaughtered animals and blood made it clear that God was very serious about His people being holy in their covenant with the holy God.

Quite soon, however, the Israelites spurned the covenant; life dwindled into habits without heart. They chose to worship wooden idols instead of adoring their living King. They didn't obey His laws of love. They didn't partner with His goodness through praying. So Father caused them to wander in the wilderness for forty years until that generation of disobedient people had passed. He swore, "They shall never enter my rest" (Ps. 95:8-11).

After forty years, a new generation finally entered the Promised Land. Sadly, they also hurt Father by challenging the covenant. Whining and stubborn, they begged to be ruled by earthly anointed kings, turning their hearts from the privilege of being ruled directly by their covenant King. Father allowed this mutiny, warning them that kings would lead them into servitude and wars. Eventually, the kingdom split into northern Israel and southern Judah, but Father continued to seek His people, conversing with the kings through prophets and visions.

Finally, God anointed David, a shepherd after His own heart, to become the king through whom Father would expand His covenant promises. God promised David that his throne and his family line would always be part of Father's planned purposes:

> I will raise up your offspring to succeed you . . .
> I will be his father, and he will be my son. When
> he does wrong, I will punish him with a rod
> wielded by men, with floggings inflicted by
> human hands. But my love will never be taken
> away from him . . . Your house and your kingdom
> will endure forever before me, your throne will be
> established forever.
>
> (2 Sam. 7:12-16)

No self-maledictory blood oath is recorded. However, the next chapter records David's *bloody battles* to subdue the nations and adds this recurring truth: "The LORD gave David victory wherever he went" (2 Sam. 8:6, 14). In response, David dedicated all the *spoils* of gold, silver and bronze to the LORD (2 Sam. 8:11).

David's passionate, mindful, covenanted love toward God is consistently recorded in the Old Testament. We read that David would *inquire of the Lord* as he faced his enemies, and he and God would converse over tactical maneuvers (2 Sam. 5:19-24). David also wrote many prayer songs to God found in the Psalms. He knew that God desires the prayers of those who love Him and obey Him. Thankfully, God even hears the prayers of penitent covenant breakers, because David was one. This is his prayer of sorrow and repentance after murdering Uriah to have Bathsheba:

> Have mercy on me, O God,
> according to your unfailing love;
> according to your great compassion
> blot out my transgressions . . . .
> Create in me a pure heart, O God,
> and renew a steadfast spirit within me.
> Do not cast me from your presence
> or take your Holy Spirit from me . . .
> You do not delight in sacrifice, or I would bring it;
> you do not take pleasure in burnt offerings.
> My sacrifice, O God, is a broken spirit;
> a broken and contrite heart
> you, God, will not despise.
>   (Ps. 51:1,10-11,16-17)

After David's death, the Old Testament records the continuing story of Israel's covenant-breaking and turning-away to follow other gods. Prophet after prophet was sent to remind God's people of His love, faithfulness, righteousness, and justice. Again and again, Father called them to repentance, but they resisted. Finally, after hundreds of years of covenant breaking, the death penalty signified by the blood oath of circumcision and the blood oath of sacrifices was coming due.

Wrathful yet gracious, Father did not sentence them to death immediately. He chose to give them even more time to turn their hearts back to Him but He uprooted them from the Promised Land, sending the Assyrians to disperse Israel and the Babylonians to destroy Jerusalem and take Judah captive (see Psalm 89). Away from home, the promises of the Old Testament—their old covenant—may have seemed null and void.

But wait! There was a *New* Testament. A *new* covenant?

Yes! Father never gave up on His children! He always keeps His promises and fulfills His covenants. As a child, I learned this rhyme often attributed in various forms to Augustine: "The New is in the Old concealed; the Old is in the New revealed." Father's prophet had announced that "a shoot will come up from the stump of Jesse; from his roots a Branch will bear fruit" (Is. 11:1). God's relationship of love with Abraham and David is an expanding and forever story!

Several hundred years of history passed without biblical record. When the New Testament opens, it presents a re-established Jewish nation teaching in synagogues and worshipping in the rebuilt Temple, but more than that, it begins with the promise that God's Son would be born as a human in the line of David! As God in the flesh, He was coming to shed His blood on the cross and take the punishment of the broken covenant upon Himself to save us.

Thanks be to Father, Son, and Holy Spirit!

Used with permission from ©brucebrownphotography

PHOTO CREDITS

Cover – Author at Pismo Beach 10/22/2017. Taken on author's camera at
    author's request.

Image 1 – Wildflowers. Highway 41 outside Pasa Robles - 12/28/2019

Image 2 – Labyrinth in Trinity Garden, Ashland, OR - 10/11/2019

Image 3 – See cover photo.

Image 4 – Feather clouds. Woodward Reservoir, Escalon, CA - 7/23/2019

Image 5 – Map created by author - journey to find car - 4/15/2021

Image 6 – Garden of Gethsemne, Mount of Olives, Israel - 3/31/2012

Image 7 – Sponge in water; author's home - 1/22/2021

Image 8 – Wall hanging purchased at Prairie Girl's Market, Missoula, MT
    9/2017 - Crafter unknown. Picture taken 9/8/2017

Image 9 – 13 - Created by C. Slager for 2019 speech - 8/23/2019

Image 14 – Pismo Beach (from Seacrest Inn property) - 12/28/2019

Image 16 – Clouds over Ripon, CA - 2/22/2017

Image 17 – Grape vines on River Road, Ripon, CA - 4/12/2020

Image 18 – Immanuel CRC steeple - 2/17/2019

Image 19 – Oregon coast - 4/9/2010

Image 20 – Wind machines, Highway 10 near Palm Springs - 1/30/2017

Image 21 – Big Trees State Park, Arnold, CA - 5/19/2018

Image 22 – American River near Sutter's Fort, Colusa, CA - 8/27/2019

Image 23 – Big tree at Kroeze cabin, Sonora, CA - 11/19/2019

Image 24 – Clouds above Highway 99 toward Sacramento - 4/16/2019

Image 25 – Rainbow over Ripon almond orchard - 2/26/2010

***

Image 15 – "Shining Down on New Life" - Oaks and sun

Image 26 – "Delta Sunrise" - Sun behind oak

Printed in the United States
by Baker & Taylor Publisher Services